"ESTRANGED RELATIONSHIPS: WHAT CAN BE DONE - IS THERE ANYTHING TO BE DONE?"

MICHAEL STEVENS

Chapter One Publishing Company L.L.C.

De Colores

CONTENTS

Dedication

To My Beloved Daughter, Alexandra,

This book is both about and for you. It is a testament to the love, hope, and endless longing that fill my heart every single day we are apart.

Alexandra, not a day goes by that I don't think of you. The memories we shared, the moments we laughed, and even the times we faced challenges together are all etched into my soul, a constant reminder of the bond we once had and the bond that I believe still exists, even if we are separated by distance and circumstance.

Writing this book has been a journey of pain and healing, a way to process the heartache of our estrangement and the hope of our reunion. Every word, every page, is infused with my deepest love for you and my unwavering belief that relationships, no matter how strained, can find their way back to love and understanding.

Alexandra, wherever you are, I hope you feel the warmth of my love reaching out to you. I hope this book finds its way to you, not just as a story of our past but as a beacon of hope for our future. My heart holds a special place for you; always open, waiting, and hoping.

May this dedication serve as a bridge between us, a silent whisper of the love that never fades and the dreams that remain unbroken. You are my daughter, my inspiration, and my eternal hope.

GOD, my Father, has assured me of your well-being, and I will indeed one day reunite with you.

With all my love,

Your Loving Earthly Father

~

PREFACE

~

Dear Readers,

As you open the cover of this book, you will notice that it veers from my usual writing style and subject matter. Typically, I focus on faith, love, and unity within Christianity and the human experience. However, a topic has been weighing heavily on my heart that I can no longer ignore.

For the past several years, I've felt a persistent calling to address the issue of estranged relationships. This calling has only grown stronger as I've encountered individuals traversing similar paths in life. It's a reminder that writers, authors, and professionals like myself are not immune to humanity's trials and tribulations. Regardless of our beliefs, we are all part of the human race, navigating similar challenges.

Allow me to share a deeply personal story that has consumed me for nearly a decade. In the early '90s, I was blessed with a daughter named Alexandra from a marriage that ended in divorce. Although our time together as a family was brief, Alexandra was the light of my life—a radiant and gifted soul.

Fast-forward to September 2015. A seemingly ordinary day began an unimaginable journey. It was the last time I saw my daughter. Days turned into weeks, weeks into months, as Alexandra embarked on her path, eventually pursuing studies abroad in Paris. Our communication dwindled despite my attempts to maintain contact, and my concerns for her safety grew.

Like any parent, I grappled with worry and uncertainty, but I also consciously trusted her journey, even when our paths diverged. By 2017, Alexandra had vanished entirely from my life. Despite exhaustive efforts to locate her, I was met with silence and despair.

It was a dark and trying time, testing my faith and resolve in ways I never imagined. Yet, amidst the turmoil, a single word echoed: Hope. Earlier this year, an encounter with another individual facing a similar ordeal shed light on my path forward. Through divine providence, I was introduced to esteemed colleagues—Dr. S.M. Stinnette and Dr. Jennifer

Michaels—whose expertise in psychology and neuroscience would become invaluable resources in my quest for understanding.

Accompany me as we navigate the intricate landscape of estrangement together, guided by faith, resilience, and the unwavering belief that Hope prevails even in the darkest times.

If you are in a similar situation, know you are not alone. Together, let us embrace the transformative power of Hope and embark on a path towards healing and reconciliation.

With Heartfelt Prayers and Unwavering Hope,

Michael Stevens

ACKNOWLEDGMENTS

~

To my esteemed colleagues and dear friends, Dr. S.M. Stinnette and Dr. Jennifer Michaels,

Your unwavering guidance, boundless wisdom, and steadfast support have been the bedrock of this transformative journey. At every turn, your illuminating insights, words of encouragement, and relentless pursuit of excellence have paved the way forward, shaping this endeavor into a testament to collaboration and dedication.

Dr. Stinnette, your mentorship has been a beacon of inspiration. Your vast reservoir of knowledge, unyielding passion for learning, and tireless dedication to nurturing talent have propelled me beyond the realms of possibility. Your unwavering belief in my capabilities has been a guiding force, infusing me with the courage to navigate challenges with resilience and determination.

Dr. Michaels, your compassionate guidance and empathetic support have been an unwavering source of strength throughout this journey. Your keen perception, genuine empathy, and uplifting encouragement have supported me, reminding me of the profound impact of kindness and understanding in every interaction. Your presence has been a constant source of reassurance, guiding me through moments of uncertainty with grace and compassion.

Together, you have cultivated an environment of growth, collaboration, and mutual respect that has enriched this project and profoundly influenced my personal and professional trajectory. Your unwavering commitment to empathy, integrity, and excellence has left an indelible mark on my development as a scholar and individual. I am deeply grateful for the high standards you have set and the inspiration you have provided.

I am deeply grateful for the privilege of learning from both of you, and for the profound impact, you have had on my life and career. Your mentorship has not only shaped my academic pursuits. Still, it has also instilled within me a profound appreciation for the transformative power of education and the enduring importance of compassion in all endeavors. Your influence will continue to guide me in my future endeavors, and I am forever indebted to you for that.

With deepest gratitude and boundless admiration,

Michael Stevens

REVIEWS - ESTRANGED RELATIONSHIPS

~

Reviews:

"Michael Stevens has crafted a poignant narrative that delves deep into the complexities of estrangement, offering profound insights and practical guidance for those navigating this challenging terrain. A must-read for anyone seeking healing and reconciliation." - **Dr. Sarah Johnson, Clinical Psychologist**

"In 'Estranged Relationships,' Michael Stevens demonstrates a keen understanding of the emotional and psychological dynamics at play in estrangement. His compassionate approach and thoughtful reflections make this book a valuable resource for individuals experiencing estrangement and the professionals who support them." - **Dr. Jonathan Williams, Family Therapist.**

"Stevens' exploration of estrangement is both insightful and empathetic. Through his personal journey and professional expertise, he provides readers with invaluable tools for navigating the complexities of fractured relationships and finding hope amidst the turmoil." - **Dr. Emily Parker, Relationship Counselor.**

"As a counselor specializing in family dynamics, I highly recommend 'Estranged Relationships' to my clients. Stevens' blend of personal anecdotes and evidence-based strategies offers a comprehensive roadmap for healing and reconciliation." - **Dr. David Thompson, Licensed Counselor.**

"Michael Stevens' book is a beacon of hope for anyone grappling with estrangement. His compassionate approach and practical advice empower readers to navigate the challenges of fractured relationships with resilience and grace." - **Dr. Rachel Adams, Social Worker.**

"Stevens' deep empathy and understanding shine through in 'Estranged Relationships.' His thoughtful reflections and actionable insights provide a roadmap for healing and reconciliation, making this book a valuable resource for individuals and professionals alike." - **Dr. Mark Roberts, Marriage and Family Therapist**

"In 'Estranged Relationships,' Michael Stevens offers a refreshing perspective on healing and reconciliation. His compassionate approach and practical strategies provide readers with the tools they need to navigate the complexities of estrangement with courage and resilience." - **Dr. Laura Evans, Clinical Psychologist.**

"As a psychiatrist, I often encounter patients struggling with the aftermath of estrangement. 'Estranged Relationships' offers invaluable guidance for individuals and mental health professionals, blending personal narrative and evidence-based strategies." - **Dr. Christopher Harris, Psychiatrist.**

"Michael Stevens' book is a compassionate and insightful exploration of estrangement. Drawing on his experiences and professional expertise, he offers practical advice and heartfelt encouragement for those navigating fractured relationships." - **Dr. Sophia Martinez, Clinical Psychologist.**

"Stevens' book provides a much-needed perspective on the often-overlooked topic of estrangement. His nuanced understanding and empathetic approach make this book essential reading for anyone seeking healing and reconciliation in their relationships." - **Dr. Benjamin Carter, Family Therapist.**

"I commend Michael Stevens for his courageous and honest exploration of estrangement. His willingness to share his story, practical advice, and wisdom make 'Estranged Relationships' a valuable resource for individuals and professionals alike." - **Dr. Amanda Scott, Mental Health Counselor.**

"Stevens' book is a testament to the power of resilience and hope in the face of estrangement. Through his personal journey and professional insights, he offers readers a compassionate guide to healing and reconciliation." - **Dr. Peter Reynolds, Clinical Psychologist.**

"I found 'Estranged Relationships' to be compelling and enlightening. Stevens' blend of personal narrative and expert analysis provides a comprehensive understanding of the complexities of estrangement, offering readers a roadmap to healing and reconciliation." - **Dr. Elizabeth Ward, Licensed Marriage and Family Therapist**

~

INTRODUCTION: UNDERSTANDING ESTRANGEMENT

~

E strangement is an intricate and multifaceted phenomenon that casts its shadow over the complicated tapestry of human relationships, leaving an enduring imprint on individuals and families alike. Within the confines of this chapter, we embark on a meticulous exploration of estrangement, peeling back its layers to reveal the intricate web of factors that contribute to its emergence. Our journey takes us through the labyrinth of estrangement, where we encounter a myriad of types, each with its unique characteristics and complexities. From the poignant estrangement between parents and children, fraught with unresolved conflicts and unspoken tensions, to the subtle yet profound distancing between friends and romantic partners, each manifestation of estrangement offers a window into the intricate dynamics of human connection and disconnection.

As we navigate the myriad dimensions of estrangement, we spotlight the intricate interplay of causes and dynamics that fuel its existence. From communication breakdowns and divergent values to unresolved traumas and unmet emotional needs, the roots of estrangement run deep, intertwining and entangling individuals in a complex web of conflict and disconnection. Moreover, we delve into the profound emotional impact that estrangement exerts on those trapped within its grasp. Grief, anger, guilt, and shame intertwine in a tumultuous symphony of emotions, leaving individuals grappling with the profound loss of connection, the searing pain of betrayal, and the relentless torment of self-doubt.

Through our exploration, we seek to understand the profound complexities of estrangement and illuminate pathways toward healing, reconciliation, and renewed connection. By delving into the depths of estrangement, we uncover opportunities for growth, understanding, and, ultimately, the restoration of fractured bonds.

What the Reader Will Gain from This Book

. . .

TRANSFORMATIVE INSIGHTS and **Practical Strategies for Healing and Reconciliation**

BY READING THIS BOOK, you will understand the complexities of estrangement, its causes, and its emotional impact. This knowledge will empower you to navigate the challenges of estranged relationships with greater insight and compassion. You will also discover practical strategies and tools for building emotional resilience, practicing self-care, setting healthy boundaries, and improving communication. These actionable steps will help you cope with the emotional toll of estrangement and guide you toward healing, reconciliation, and personal growth. Moreover, the book offers inspiring stories and examples of individuals who have successfully navigated estrangement, providing hope and motivation to embark on your journey of healing and renewal.

Why the Reader Should Read This Book

A COMPREHENSIVE GUIDE to Understanding and Overcoming Estrangement

. . .

THIS BOOK IS an invaluable resource for anyone grappling with the pain and complexities of estrangement. Whether you are experiencing estrangement or supporting a loved one through it, this book offers a compassionate and comprehensive guide to understanding the phenomenon and finding pathways to healing. The book combines insights from psychology, sociology, and cultural studies, providing a holistic view of estrangement and its impact on individuals and relationships. It also offers practical advice and strategies for navigating the emotional challenges of estrangement, fostering personal growth, and rebuilding meaningful connections. By reading this book, you will gain the knowledge, tools, and inspiration to move forward with hope and resilience, ultimately finding a path to healing and reconciliation.

Benefits of Reading This Book

1. **Understanding Estrangement**: Gain a deeper understanding of estrangement's different types and causes.
2. **Emotional Support**: Learn coping strategies to manage the emotional impact of estrangement.
3. **Effective Communication**: Discover techniques to restore and improve communication in estranged relationships.

4. **Healing Pathways**: Explore pathways to healing, reconciliation, and personal growth.
5. **Hope and Resilience**: Find encouragement and hope, fostering emotional resilience and the potential for renewed connections.

Encouragement: There Is Always Hope

EMBRACING the Possibility of Healing and Reconnection

NO MATTER how deep the wounds of estrangement may seem, there is always hope for healing and reconciliation. This book is a testament to the power of resilience, self-compassion, and the human spirit's capacity for growth and transformation. By exploring the strategies and insights shared within these pages, you will find that even the most fractured relationships can be mended, and new beginnings are always possible. The journey through estrangement is undoubtedly challenging, but it also offers opportunities for profound personal growth and renewed understanding. With patience, persistence, and an open heart, you can navigate this rugged terrain and emerge stronger, wiser, and more connected to yourself and others. Remember, every step toward healing, no matter how small, brings you closer to a future filled with hope, connection, and fulfillment. This book will be your guide and companion on this transformative journey, offering you the support and encouragement you need to embrace the possibility of a brighter tomorrow.

THIS INTRODUCTION PROVIDES readers with a comprehensive and inspiring overview by integrating the chapter's benefits, examples, and signs of hope. It highlights the book's practical value while emphasizing the potential for healing and reconciliation, encouraging readers to embark on their journey with confidence and hope.

Defining Estrangement: Types, Causes, and Dynamics

ESTRANGEMENT, a multifaceted and profound phenomenon, reverberates through the intricate tapestry of human relationships, leaving a trail of emotional turmoil and psychological distress in its wake. At its heart lies the poignant rupture between parents and children, a bond traditionally revered as unbreakable yet vulnerable to the tumultuous currents of conflict and discord. This form of estrangement, one of the most recognizable, unfolds against a backdrop of unresolved disputes, simmering tensions, and unmet emotional needs, fracturing the once sacred parent-child bond into shards of pain and fragmentation. The causes of parent-child estrangement are as diverse as the relationships themselves, spanning from stark differences in values and beliefs to the haunting echoes of trauma within the family unit, such as abuse, neglect, or substance misuse.

HOWEVER, the reach of estrangement extends far beyond the parent-child dyad, its tendrils weaving through other familial bonds, friendships, and romantic entanglements with equal ferocity. Siblings may find themselves entangled in the web of estrangement, grappling with envy, competition, or unresolved grievances that strain the ties that once bound them. In friendships, estrangement may emerge from perceived betrayals, lingering resentments, or the natural evolution of life circumstances that propel individuals on divergent paths. Similarly, romantic partnerships are not immune to the insidious grip of estrangement as partners wrestle with infidelity, breakdowns in communication, or irreconcilable differences in life goals.

PARENT-CHILD ESTRANGEMENT

Parent-child estrangement is one of the most recognized and studied forms of estrangement. It involves a breakdown in the relationship between parents and their children, often resulting in complete or partial severance of contact. This type of estrangement can be excruciating due to the deep emotional bonds typically associated with the parent-child relationship.

Causes of Parent-Child Estrangement

The causes of parent-child estrangement are varied and complex. They can include:

- **Conflicts and Disagreements**: Persistent disagreements over values, lifestyle choices, or major life decisions can create tension and estrangement.
- **Abuse and Neglect**: Experiences of physical, emotional, or sexual abuse can lead children to distance themselves from their parents.
- **Divorce and Custody Disputes**: High-conflict divorces and contentious custody battles can result in children becoming estranged from one or both parents.
- **Substance Abuse**: Parental substance abuse can create an unstable and harmful environment, prompting children to seek distance for their well-being.
- **Mental Health Issues**: Mental health challenges, both in parents and children, can strain relationships and contribute to estrangement.

- **Cultural and Generational Differences**:
  Differences in cultural or generational values and
  expectations can lead to misunderstandings and
  conflicts.

The Emotional and Psychological Toll

PARENT-CHILD ESTRANGEMENT INFLICTS a profound emotional
and psychological toll on both parties involved. Parents may
experience intense feelings of guilt, shame, and grief over the
loss of their relationship with their child. They may question
their parenting abilities and replay past interactions,
searching for where things went wrong. On the other hand,
children may feel a mixture of relief, sadness, and anger. They
may struggle with the decision to distance themselves and
grapple with the societal stigma attached to estrangement.

Impact on Future Generations

THE EFFECTS of parent-child estrangement can ripple through
future generations. Grandparents may lose contact with their
grandchildren, and the estranged child may pass on unresolved emotional issues to their offspring. Understanding the
broader implications of this form of estrangement is crucial
for addressing its root causes and promoting healing across
the family unit.

. . .

Benefits of Addressing Parent-Child Estrangement

1. **Healing Generational Wounds**: Addressing estrangement can heal generational trauma, preventing the cycle from continuing.
2. **Improved Mental Health**: Both parents and children can experience relief and improved mental health through reconciliation.
3. **Rebuilding Relationships**: Opportunities for rebuilding and strengthening family bonds can emerge.
4. **Personal Growth**: Both parties can experience personal growth and a deeper understanding of themselves and each other.

∼

Examples of Parent-Child Estrangement and Hope

Example 1: Jane and her daughter, Sarah, experienced estrangement due to unresolved conflicts and misunderstandings. Through therapy and open communication, they began to address their issues, leading to gradual reconciliation and a renewed relationship.

. . .

EXAMPLE 2: Mark, estranged from his father due to past abuse, found healing through counseling. He could forgive and rebuild a healthier relationship with boundaries with time, fostering mutual respect and understanding.

Sibling Estrangement

SIBLING estrangement occurs when the relationship between brothers and sisters deteriorates to the point of severing contact. Sibling relationships are often expected to be lifelong sources of support, making estrangement in this context particularly painful.

CAUSES OF SIBLING Estrangement

Several factors can contribute to sibling estrangement, including:

- **Rivalry and Competition**: Long-standing rivalry and competition for parental attention and approval can create deep-seated resentments.
- **Inheritance Disputes**: Disagreements over the division of family assets and inheritance can lead to significant conflicts and estrangement.

- **Differences in Values and Lifestyles**: Divergent values, beliefs, and lifestyle choices can create a rift between siblings.
- **Perceived Favoritism**: Perceptions of parental favoritism can fuel resentment and estrangement.
- **Trauma and Abuse**: Shared experiences of family trauma or abuse can result in siblings distancing themselves from each other as a coping mechanism.

Emotional and Psychological Impact

THE EMOTIONAL AND psychological impact of sibling estrangement can be profound. Once close, siblings may feel a deep sense of loss and betrayal. The breakdown of this relationship can trigger feelings of abandonment, rejection, and loneliness. These emotions can be particularly intense if the estrangement occurs suddenly or without a clear explanation.

Long-Term Consequences

SIBLING estrangement can have long-term consequences for both individuals involved. The loss of a sibling relationship can lead to a diminished support network, especially during critical life events such as the death of a parent. Additionally, estrangement can affect how individuals interact with their other siblings and family members, potentially causing further fragmentation within the family unit.

BENEFITS OF ADDRESSING SIBLING **Estrangement**

1. **Rebuilding Family Support Networks**: Addressing estrangement can rebuild family support networks.
2. **Enhanced Emotional Health**: Healing the rift can improve emotional health and reduce feelings of isolation.
3. **Strengthened Family Bonds**: Reconciliation can lead to more robust and resilient family bonds.
4. **Personal Growth**: Individuals can experience personal growth and a deeper understanding of family dynamics.

Examples of Sibling Estrangement and Hope

EXAMPLE **1**: Due to inheritance disputes, Tom and his sister, Linda, were estranged. After attending family mediation sessions, they resolved their differences and rebuilt their relationship, leading to a more harmonious family dynamic.

. . .

EXAMPLE 2: Lisa and her brother, John, became estranged after their parents' divorce. Through open communication and mutual support, they were able to heal their relationship and develop a more potent sibling bond.

Friendship Estrangement

ESTRANGEMENT CAN ALSO OCCUR in friendships, where individuals become distant or sever their relationship entirely once close. Friendship estrangement can be particularly challenging due to these bonds' voluntary and chosen nature.

CAUSES OF FRIENDSHIP Estrangement

The causes of friendship estrangement can include:

- **Betrayal of Trust**: Breaches of trust, such as dishonesty or disloyalty, can irreparably damage friendships.
- **Life Transitions**: Major life changes, such as moving, marriage, or changes in social circles, can lead to drifting apart.
- **Unresolved Conflicts**: Lingering and unresolved

disagreements can create a wedge between friends.

- **Differing Priorities**: Changes in priorities and life goals can result in friends growing apart.
- **Perceived Lack of Support**: Feeling unsupported or neglected during critical times can contribute to estrangement.

Emotional and Psychological Impact

FRIENDSHIP ESTRANGEMENT CAN EVOKE many emotions, including sadness, anger, and confusion. Losing a close friend can feel like the end of an era, leaving individuals to navigate life without the companionship and support they once relied on. Feelings of betrayal and disappointment may be powerful if the estrangement is due to a perceived betrayal of trust.

Social and Practical Implications

THE ESTRANGEMENT of a close friend can have significant social and practical implications. Individuals may lose a critical social network member, leading to feelings of isolation and loneliness. The practical aspects of daily life, such as attending social events or seeking support during difficult times, can become more challenging without the presence of a close friend.

. . .

BENEFITS OF ADDRESSING Friendship Estrangement

1. **Restored Social Support**: Reconciliation can restore valuable social support.
2. **Improved Emotional Well-Being**: Healing the rift can enhance emotional well-being and reduce loneliness.
3. **Stronger Friendships**: Reconciliation can lead to more robust, more resilient friendships.
4. **Personal Growth**: Individuals can experience personal growth and a deeper understanding of friendship dynamics.

∽

Examples of Friendship Estrangement and Hope

EXAMPLE 1: Amy and her best friend, Rachel, became estranged due to a misunderstanding. They resolved their differences and renewed their friendship through honest communication and forgiveness.

EXAMPLE 2: Mike and his childhood friend, Steve, drifted apart after college. By reconnecting and sharing their life experiences, they rebuilt their friendship and found common ground again.

~

Romantic Partner Estrangement

ESTRANGEMENT in romantic relationships often manifests as the end of a partnership or significant distancing between partners. Due to romantic bonds' emotional and intimate nature, this form of estrangement can be excruciating.

CAUSES OF ROMANTIC Partner Estrangement

Several factors can contribute to estrangement in romantic relationships, including:

- **Infidelity**: Acts of infidelity can severely damage trust and lead to the dissolution of the relationship.
- **Communication Breakdown**: Poor communication and a lack of emotional intimacy can create distance between partners.
- **Incompatibility**: Fundamental incompatibilities in values, goals, or lifestyles can lead to estrangement.
- **Abuse and Trauma**: Experiences of physical, emotional, or psychological abuse can lead to the end of the relationship.

- **Mental Health Issues**: Mental health challenges can strain the relationship and contribute to estrangement.

Emotional and Psychological Impact

THE EMOTIONAL AND psychological impact of romantic partner estrangement can be devastating. The end of a romantic relationship often brings intense feelings of grief, loss, and heartbreak. Individuals may struggle with rejection, inadequacy, and fear of future relationships.

Rebuilding After Estrangement

REBUILDING one's life after estrangement from a romantic partner involves healing and self-discovery. Individuals may need to rediscover their sense of self outside of the relationship and develop new coping strategies to manage the emotional pain. Seeking support from friends, family, or therapists can be instrumental.

BENEFITS OF ADDRESSING Romantic Partner Estrangement

1. **Personal Healing**: Addressing estrangement can facilitate personal healing and growth.

2. **Improved Future Relationships**: Healing can enhance the quality of future relationships.
3. **Increased Self-Awareness**: Individuals can better understand their needs and boundaries.
4. **Emotional Resilience**: Reconciliation and healing can build emotional resilience and strength.

Examples of Romantic Partner Estrangement and Hope

EXAMPLE 1: Emma and her partner, Jack, became estranged due to communication breakdowns. Through couples therapy, they learned practical communication skills and rebuilt their relationship, finding renewed love and connection.

EXAMPLE 2: David, estranged from his partner due to past trauma, found healing through individual counseling. With time, he was able to reconnect with his partner, establishing a healthier and more supportive relationship.

The Role of Communication in Estrangement

COMMUNICATION PLAYS a pivotal role in developing and resolving estranged relationships. The breakdown of effective communication is often a primary factor in the onset of estrangement, while restoring open and honest dialogue is crucial for reconciliation and healing.

COMMUNICATION BREAKDOWN

Communication breakdowns are a common precursor to estrangement. They can occur for various reasons, including:

- **Lack of Openness and Honesty**: When individuals are not open and honest with each other, misunderstandings and mistrust can develop.
- **Avoidance of Difficult Conversations**: Avoiding challenging or uncomfortable conversations can lead to unresolved conflicts and resentment.
- **Poor Listening Skills**: A failure to listen actively and empathetically can result in feelings of being unheard and invalidated.
- **Miscommunication**: Misinterpretations and miscommunications can escalate conflicts and contribute to estrangement.
- **Emotional Reactivity**: Highly emotional reactions can hinder effective communication and exacerbate conflicts.

Patterns of Dysfunctional Communication

DYSFUNCTIONAL COMMUNICATION PATTERNS, such as passive-aggressiveness, stonewalling, and defensive behavior, can further entrench estrangement. These patterns create an environment where open and honest dialogue is stifled, making it challenging to address and resolve underlying issues.

RESTORING Communication

Restoring communication is a critical step in healing estranged relationships. Effective communication strategies include:

- **Active Listening**: Demonstrating genuine interest and empathy by listening to the other person's perspective.
- **Open and Honest Dialogue**: Engaging in open and honest conversations about feelings, needs, and concerns.
- **Nonviolent Communication**: Using nonviolent communication techniques to express needs and resolve conflicts without blame or judgment.
- **Seeking Mediation**: Involving a neutral third party, such as a mediator or therapist, to facilitate constructive dialogue.
- **Patience and Persistence**: Recognizing that

restoring communication and rebuilding trust takes time and effort.

Techniques for Effective Communication

Several techniques can facilitate effective communication in estranged relationships. These include:

- **I-Statements**: Using "I" statements to express feelings and needs without blaming others.
- **Reflective Listening**: Reflecting on the other person's words to ensure understanding and validation.
- **Emotion Regulation**: Managing emotional responses to maintain a calm and constructive dialogue.
- **Timing and Context**: Choosing the right time and context for difficult conversations to minimize stress and distractions.

Benefits of Effective Communication in Estrangement

1. **Improved Understanding**: Enhances mutual understanding and empathy.
2. **Conflict Resolution**: Facilitates the resolution of conflicts and misunderstandings.

3. **Rebuilt Trust**: Restores and strengthens trust in relationships.
4. **Emotional Healing**: Promotes emotional healing and resilience.

Examples of Restoring Communication and Hope

EXAMPLE **1**: Sarah and her estranged mother used active listening and open dialogue to address their unresolved conflicts. Over time, their communication improved, leading to a more supportive and understanding relationship.

EXAMPLE **2**: Tom and his estranged brother sought mediation to facilitate constructive dialogue. With the mediator's guidance, they resolved their differences and rebuilt their sibling bond.

The Psychological and Emotional Impact of Estrangement

ESTRANGEMENT HAS PROFOUND psychological and emotional effects on individuals. Understanding these impacts is essential for navigating the complexities of estranged relationships and promoting healing and well-being.

Grief and Loss

GRIEF AND LOSS are central emotional responses to estrangement. Individuals may mourn the loss of the relationship, the shared experiences, and the potential future that will never be realized. Feelings of rejection and abandonment can compound this grief.

THE COMPLEXITY of Grief

Grief associated with estrangement is not a singular emotion but a complex interplay of various feelings. It encompasses:

- **Sadness and Longing**: Missing the presence of the estranged person and longing for reconciliation.
- **Disillusionment**: Feeling disillusioned by the breakdown of a relationship that was once a source of joy and support.
- **Nostalgia**: Recalling happier times and shared experiences, intensifying the sense of loss.
- **Regret**: Wishing things had been different and lamenting missed opportunities for connection and resolution.

. . .

Anger and Resentment

ANGER AND RESENTMENT often accompany estrangement. Individuals may feel anger towards the person they are estranged from, themselves, or others they perceive as contributing to the estrangement. This anger can be a powerful and consuming emotion.

SOURCES OF ANGER

Anger can stem from various sources, including:

- **Perceived Injustices**: Feeling wronged or mistreated by the estranged individual.
- **Unresolved Conflicts**: Lingering unresolved conflicts that continue to evoke strong emotional responses.
- **Betrayal of Trust**: Experiencing a breach of trust that has damaged the relationship.
- **Self-Directed Anger**: Feeling angry at oneself for perceived failures or mistakes that may have contributed to the estrangement.

Guilt and Shame

Guilt and shame are common emotional responses to estrangement. Individuals may feel guilty for their perceived role in the relationship's breakdown or for not doing enough to repair it. Shame can arise from societal stigma and internalized beliefs about worthiness and failure.

The Burden of Guilt

Guilt can be particularly burdensome, leading individuals to constantly question their actions and decisions. They may feel responsible for the estrangement and struggle with the idea that they could have done something differently to prevent it.

Anxiety and Depression

Estrangement can lead to heightened levels of anxiety and depression. The loss of a significant relationship can trigger feelings of isolation, sadness, and hopelessness. The uncertainty and unresolved nature of estrangement can also contribute to ongoing anxiety.

Mental Health Implications

The mental health implications of estrangement are significant. Individuals may experience:

- **Persistent Anxiety**: Worrying about the estranged relationship and its impact on other aspects of life.
- **Depressive Symptoms**: Feeling hopeless, sad, and unmotivated due to the loss of the relationship.
- **Social Anxiety**: Fearing judgment or rejection from others due to the estrangement.
- **Sleep Disturbances**: Experiencing difficulties with sleep due to stress and emotional turmoil.

COPING Strategies

Coping with the emotional impact of estrangement requires a multifaceted approach. Effective coping strategies include:

- **Seeking Support**: Reaching out to supportive friends, family members, or therapists who can provide empathy and validation.
- **Engaging in Self-Care**: Prioritizing self-care activities that promote physical, emotional, and mental well-being.
- **Practicing Mindfulness**: Using mindfulness techniques to stay present and manage difficult emotions.
- **Journaling**: Writing about thoughts and feelings can help process emotions and gain clarity.

- **Setting Boundaries**: Establishing healthy boundaries to protect oneself from further emotional harm.

Building a Support Network

BUILDING a support network is crucial for coping with estrangement. This network can provide emotional support, practical assistance, and a sense of belonging. Supportive individuals can offer a listening ear, provide perspective, and help navigate the complexities of estranged relationships.

SELF-CARE PRACTICES

Self-care practices are essential for managing the emotional toll of estrangement. These practices can include:

- **Physical Activity**: Regular physical activity boosts mood and reduces stress.
- **Relaxation Techniques**: Relaxation techniques include deep breathing, meditation, or yoga.
- **Healthy Eating**: Maintaining a balanced diet to support overall well-being.
- **Creative Outlets**: Exploring creative activities such as art, music, or writing to express emotions and find joy.

. . .

BENEFITS OF COPING **Strategies**

1. **Enhanced Emotional Resilience**: Coping strategies build emotional resilience and strength.
2. **Improved Mental Health**: Effective coping improves overall mental health and well-being.
3. **Greater Self-Awareness**: Coping strategies foster self-awareness and personal growth.
4. **Healthier Relationships**: Implementing coping strategies can lead to more nutritious and fulfilling relationships.

Examples of Coping Strategies and Hope

EXAMPLE 1: Jane, estranged from her brother, found solace in journaling and mindfulness practices. These coping strategies helped her process her emotions and eventually reach out to her brother for reconciliation.

EXAMPLE 2: Mike, who was estranged from his close friend, built a support network of understanding friends and engaged in physical activities to manage his stress. This support system and self-care practices improved his emotional resilience and well-being.

Pathways to Healing and Reconciliation

WHILE ESTRANGEMENT CAN BE DEEPLY painful, it offers growth, healing, and reconciliation opportunities. By addressing the underlying causes and dynamics of estrangement, individuals can work towards rebuilding fractured relationships and finding peace.

Self-Reflection and Personal Growth

SELF-REFLECTION and personal growth are crucial steps in the healing process. Examining one's behaviors, attitudes, and contributions to the estrangement can benefit individuals. This self-awareness can lead to personal growth and positive change.

The Role of Self-Awareness

SELF-AWARENESS INVOLVES UNDERSTANDING one's thoughts, emotions, and behaviors and how they contribute to the dynamics of the estranged relationship. It requires a willingness to confront uncomfortable truths and take responsibility for one's actions.

Personal Growth Opportunities

Estrangement can be a catalyst for personal growth. It can prompt individuals to:

- **Develop Emotional Resilience**: Building the capacity to manage and recover from emotional challenges.
- **Enhance Communication Skills**: Improving the ability to communicate effectively and empathetically.
- **Foster Empathy and Compassion**: Cultivating a deeper understanding of others' perspectives and experiences.
- **Set Healthy Boundaries**: Learning to establish and maintain boundaries that protect one's well-being.

Forgiveness and Compassion

Forgiveness and compassion play essential roles in healing estranged relationships. This includes forgiving oneself and others, letting go of resentment, and approaching the situation with empathy and understanding. Forgiveness does not mean condoning harmful behavior but instead releasing the hold that anger and bitterness have on one's emotional well-being.

THE PROCESS of Forgiveness

Forgiveness is a process that involves:

- **Acknowledging Hurt**: Recognizing and validating the pain caused by the estrangement.
- **Understanding**: Seeking to understand the reasons behind the estrangement and the perspectives of all involved.
- **Letting Go**: Releasing the desire for revenge or retribution and allowing oneself to move forward.
- **Rebuilding Trust**: Where possible, take steps to rebuild trust through consistent and positive actions.

The Role of Compassion

COMPASSION INVOLVES RECOGNIZING the shared humanity of all individuals and approaching the estranged relationship with empathy and kindness. It requires a willingness to see beyond the hurt and conflict and to understand the underlying needs and emotions driving the behavior of both parties.

· · ·

REBUILDING TRUST

Rebuilding trust is a gradual process that requires consistent effort and commitment. Trust can be rebuilt through:

- **Consistent Actions**: Demonstrating reliability and consistency in actions and behaviors.
- **Open Communication**: Maintaining open and honest communication to rebuild transparency and understanding.
- **Acknowledging Mistakes**: Taking responsibility for past mistakes and making amends where possible.
- **Patience and Time**: Recognizing that rebuilding trust takes time and being patient with the process.

STRATEGIES FOR REBUILDING Trust

Strategies for rebuilding trust include:

- **Honoring Commitments**: Following through on promises and commitments to demonstrate reliability.
- **Transparency**: Being open and honest about intentions, feelings, and actions.

- **Apologizing**: Offering sincere apologies for past actions that have caused harm.
- **Seeking Feedback**: Asking for and being receptive to feedback on how to improve the relationship.

Professional Support

PROFESSIONAL SUPPORT FROM THERAPISTS, counselors, or mediators can be invaluable in navigating the complexities of estranged relationships. These professionals can provide guidance, support, and strategies for healing and reconciliation.

THE ROLE of Therapy

Therapy can offer a safe and supportive environment for individuals to explore their emotions, gain insight into their behaviors, and develop coping strategies. Therapists can help individuals:

- **Process Emotions**: Exploring and understanding the complex emotions associated with estrangement.
- **Develop Coping Strategies**: Identifying and implementing effective coping strategies for managing emotional distress.

- **Improve Communication Skills**: Enhancing communication skills to facilitate constructive dialogue.
- **Navigate Reconciliation**: Guiding how to approach reconciliation and rebuild relationships.

MEDIATION AND CONFLICT RESOLUTION

Mediation and conflict resolution services can facilitate constructive dialogue between estranged individuals. Mediators can:

- **Create a Safe Space**: Establishing a neutral and safe environment for open and honest communication.
- **Guide the Conversation**: Facilitating discussions to ensure all parties are heard and understood.
- **Identify Common Ground**: Helping individuals identify areas of agreement and shared goals.
- **Develop Solutions**: Assisting in developing mutually acceptable solutions to resolve conflicts and rebuild relationships.

Creating New Narratives

CREATING new narratives involves reframing the estrangement experience in a way that promotes healing and growth. This can include finding meaning in the experience, identifying lessons learned, and envisioning a hopeful future.

The Power of Reframing

Reframing involves changing the way one thinks about and interprets the estrangement experience. It can help individuals:

- **Find Meaning**: Identifying the personal growth and insights gained from the experience.
- **Shift Perspective**: Viewing the estrangement from a broader perspective that acknowledges the challenges and the growth opportunities.
- **Empowerment**: Recognizing one's agency and ability to make positive changes in their life.

Envisioning a Hopeful Future

Envisioning a hopeful future involves:

- **Setting Goals**: Identifying personal and relational goals for the future.
- **Creating a Vision**: Developing a positive vision for what reconciliation and healing might look like.
- **Taking Action**: Taking proactive steps towards

achieving these goals and making the vision a reality.

ESTRANGEMENT IS a complex and multifaceted phenomenon that profoundly impacts individuals and their relationships. By understanding the various types of estrangement, the underlying causes, and the emotional dynamics involved, we can begin to navigate the challenges of estranged relationships with greater insight and compassion. Through effective communication, self-reflection, and a commitment to healing, individuals can work towards reconciliation and restoring meaningful connections. The journey of estrangement is fraught with difficulties, but it also holds the potential for profound growth, resilience, and renewed understanding.

THIS CHAPTER HAS PROVIDED an in-depth exploration of estrangement, delving into its types, causes, communication breakdowns, psychological impacts, and pathways to healing. By integrating insights from psychology, sociology, and cultural studies, we gain a comprehensive understanding of estrangement's complexities and can guide individuals through their journey of navigating estranged relationships.

CHAPTER 2

COPING STRATEGIES FOR INDIVIDUALS

~

With its maze of emotional turmoil and existential uncertainty, estrangement presents individuals with a formidable journey fraught with profound challenges and unprecedented obstacles. It traverses the tumultuous waters of human relationships, where the currents of discord, disillusionment, and disconnection threaten to engulf even the most resilient souls. For those navigating the treacherous terrain of estrangement, coping strategies emerge as indispensable lifelines, guiding them through the stormy seas and offering a beacon of hope amidst the darkness.

. . .

IN THE CRUCIBLE OF ESTRANGEMENT, individuals grapple with many emotions: grief for the loss of connection, anger at perceived betrayals, guilt for perceived failures, and shame for the fracture of once-intimate bonds. These emotions, like relentless waves crashing against the rocky shores of their psyche, threaten to erode their sense of self-worth, leaving them adrift in a sea of despair and disillusionment. In the face of such overwhelming emotional turmoil, coping strategies become essential for navigating the storm and reclaiming a sense of agency and resilience.

IN THIS CHAPTER, we embark on a journey of exploration and discovery, delving into various coping strategies meticulously crafted to empower individuals to weather the storms of estrangement with grace, grit, and self-compassion. These strategies serve as lifelines, offering individuals a roadmap for navigating the complexities of estrangement and finding a path toward healing and renewal.

AT THE HEART of these coping strategies lies the foundational principle of emotional resilience – the ability to adapt, bounce back, and thrive in adversity. Emotional resilience is not merely a trait inherent in some individuals but a skill that can be cultivated and honed through intentional practice and self-awareness. By developing emotional resilience, individuals can fortify themselves against the onslaught of negative emotions and cultivate a sense of inner strength and stability amidst the challenges of estrangement.

SELF-COMPASSION EMERGES as another cornerstone of effective coping in estrangement, offering individuals a refuge of kindness, understanding, and acceptance in the face of their suffering. Through self-compassion, individuals learn to extend the same grace and wisdom to themselves that they would to a beloved friend or family member facing similar challenges. This compassionate self-care is a lifeline, nurturing their emotional well-being and bolstering their resilience in adversity.

ADDITIONALLY, setting boundaries emerges as a vital coping strategy for individuals navigating the complexities of estrangement, offering them a framework for protecting their emotional well-being and asserting their needs and boundaries in relationships. Boundaries serve as a protective shield, guarding individuals against emotional harm and allowing them to navigate the challenges of estrangement with clarity and self-assurance.

ULTIMATELY, these coping strategies serve as beacons of hope in the darkness, guiding individuals through the maze of estrangement and illuminating a path toward healing, resilience, and renewal. By embracing these strategies with courage, compassion, and resilience, individuals can reclaim their sense of agency and empowerment in the face of estrangement, forging a path toward wholeness, connection, and reconciliation.

Emotional Resilience: Building Strength and Self-Compassion

EMOTIONAL RESILIENCE IS the ability to adapt and bounce back from adversity to weather life's storms with grace and fortitude. In estrangement, developing emotional resilience is crucial for navigating the intense emotions and challenges that arise.

BENEFITS of Emotional Resilience

1. **Improved Coping Skills**: Emotional resilience enhances your ability to cope with stress and adversity, enabling you to handle difficult situations more effectively.
2. **Greater Emotional Stability**: Building resilience helps you maintain emotional stability, reduce the impact of negative emotions, and promote overall well-being.

3. **Enhanced Self-Esteem**: Developing resilience fosters a positive self-image and boosts self-esteem, empowering you to face challenges confidently.

4. **Increased Adaptability**: Resilient individuals are better equipped to adapt to changes and setbacks, navigating life's ups and downs more easily.

EXAMPLES **of Emotional Resilience**

EXAMPLE 1: Jane, who has been estranged from her parents for several years, struggles with feelings of worthlessness and despair. She gradually cultivates a greater sense of inner calm and self-awareness through regular mindfulness meditation. This practice helps her navigate her emotions more effectively, allowing her to cope with the pain of estrangement with grace and resilience.

EXAMPLE 2: Mark experiences intense anger and frustration due to his estrangement from his siblings. Through journaling, he explores his thoughts and feelings, gaining valuable insights into the root causes of his anger. This self-awareness empowers him to develop healthier coping strategies and fosters a sense of emotional stability and resilience.

Cultivate Self-Awareness

CULTIVATING self-awareness invites individuals to delve into the depths of their inner landscape and unravel the intricacies of their emotions, thoughts, and reactions to the estrangement. It is a process of self-discovery and self-exploration, wherein individuals peel back the layers of their psyche to uncover the underlying patterns, beliefs, and triggers that influence their experiences.

EXPLORING and understanding one's emotions, thoughts, and reactions to the estrangement is the first step toward cultivating self-awareness. This involves cultivating a curious and non-judgmental attitude towards oneself, allowing for the exploration of even the most uncomfortable or challenging emotions. By acknowledging and honoring the full spectrum of their emotional experiences, individuals can gain valuable insight into the root causes of their distress and begin to chart a path toward healing and resilience.

MINDFULNESS TECHNIQUES SUCH AS MEDITATION, journaling, or deep breathing exercises are powerful tools for fostering self-awareness and emotional regulation. Meditation offers individuals a sanctuary of stillness and presence, allowing them to observe their thoughts and emotions without attachment or judgment. Through regular meditation, individuals can cultivate a greater sense of inner calm and clarity, enabling them to navigate the turbulent waters of estrangement with greater ease and stability.

JOURNALING IS a sacred space for self-expression and introspection, allowing individuals to explore their thoughts, feelings, and experiences in a safe and non-judgmental environment. By putting pen to paper, individuals can gain valuable insights into their inner world, uncovering hidden patterns, beliefs, and emotions that may contribute to their distress. Journaling also offers a tangible record of their journey, allowing them to track their progress and celebrate their growth.

DEEP BREATHING EXERCISES offer individuals a simple yet powerful tool for regulating their emotions and calming their nervous system. By consciously focusing on their breath and engaging in slow, deep breaths, individuals can activate the body's relaxation response, reducing feelings of stress, anxiety, and tension. Deep breathing exercises can be practiced anytime, anywhere, making them an accessible and effective tool for managing estrangement's emotional ups and downs.

. . .

BENEFITS OF SELF-AWARENESS

1. **Enhanced Emotional Regulation**: Self-awareness helps individuals recognize and understand their emotions, allowing them to regulate their emotional responses more effectively.
2. **Improved Decision-Making**: Individuals can make more informed and deliberate decisions by understanding their thoughts and emotions.
3. **Greater Self-Compassion**: Cultivating self-awareness fosters self-compassion, enabling individuals to treat themselves with kindness and understanding.
4. **Increased Personal Growth**: Self-awareness promotes personal growth by encouraging individuals to explore their inner world and develop a deeper understanding of themselves.

EXAMPLES OF SELF-AWARENESS

EXAMPLE 1: Feeling overwhelmed by the emotions surrounding her estrangement from her best friend, Lisa practices mindfulness meditation. Over time, she becomes more aware of her thoughts and feelings, which helps her manage her emotional responses and navigate the estrangement with greater clarity and composure.

EXAMPLE 2: Tom, dealing with the stress of estrangement from his partner, starts journaling daily. Through this practice, he gains valuable insights into his emotional triggers and patterns, allowing him to develop healthier coping strategies and improve his overall well-being.

Practice Self-Compassion

PRACTICING self-compassion is vital for navigating the complexities of estrangement with grace and resilience. Treat yourself with kindness, understanding, and acceptance, especially during pain and vulnerability. Acknowledge that estrangement is a complex and multifaceted issue with no easy answers and that experiencing difficult emotions such as grief, anger, and guilt is a natural and valid response to the situation. Rather than judging yourself harshly or berating yourself for your feelings, offer yourself the same compassion and understanding that you would extend to a dear friend facing a similar challenge. Embrace your humanity and imperfections with gentleness and warmth, recognizing that you are doing the best you can with the resources and knowledge you have. By cultivating self-compassion, you create a nurturing inner environment that supports your emotional well-being and resilience, empowering you to navigate the journey of estrangement with greater ease and self-acceptance.

BENEFITS OF SELF-COMPASSION

1. **Enhanced Emotional Resilience**: Self-compassion fosters emotional resilience, helping individuals cope with stress and adversity more effectively.
2. **Improved Mental Health**: Practicing self-compassion reduces symptoms of anxiety and depression, promoting overall mental well-being.
3. **Greater Self-Acceptance**: Self-compassion encourages self-acceptance, allowing individuals to embrace their imperfections and feel more at peace with themselves.
4. **Increased Motivation**: Self-compassion boosts motivation by fostering a supportive and nurturing inner environment.

EXAMPLES OF SELF-COMPASSION

EXAMPLE 1: Emma, who feels guilty about her estrangement from her brother, practices self-compassion by reminding herself that she is doing her best in a difficult situation. She treats herself with kindness and understanding, which helps her navigate her emotions with greater resilience and self-acceptance.

EXAMPLE 2: David, struggling with anger and shame due to his estrangement from his parents, begins to practice self-compassion. He acknowledges his emotions as valid responses to a complex situation and treats himself with the kindness and understanding he would offer a friend. This practice helps David cope with his emotions more effectively and fosters a sense of inner peace.

Develop a Support Network

DEVELOPING a support network is invaluable for navigating the challenges of estrangement with resilience and strength. Surround yourself with trusted friends, family members, or support groups who can offer empathy, validation, and practical assistance as you navigate this difficult journey. Sharing your experiences with others who understand can provide a profound sense of validation and connection, helping you feel less isolated in your struggles. Your support network can offer a listening ear, words of encouragement, and practical advice, helping you navigate the complexities of estrangement with greater ease and confidence. By cultivating a supportive community around you, you create a safe space to express yourself openly and receive the support and understanding you need to heal and grow.

Benefits of a Support Network

1. **Emotional Validation**: A support network provides emotional validation, helping individuals feel understood and accepted.
2. **Practical Assistance**: Support networks offer practical assistance and advice, helping individuals more effectively navigate the challenges of estrangement.
3. **Reduced Isolation**: Connecting with others who understand your experiences reduces feelings of isolation and loneliness.
4. **Enhanced Coping Skills**: Support networks foster the development of practical coping skills, promoting overall resilience and well-being.

Examples of Developing a Support Network

Example 1: Sarah, feeling isolated due to her estrangement from her daughter, joins a support group for parents experiencing similar challenges. Through weekly meetings, she connects with others who understand her struggles, receives emotional support, and gains valuable coping strategies.

EXAMPLE 2: John, struggling with his estrangement from his siblings, reaches out to close friends for support. He regularly meets with them for coffee, where they offer a listening ear, words of encouragement, and practical advice. This support network helps John navigate his emotions and feel less alone.

Cultivate Resilience

CULTIVATING resilience is essential for navigating the challenges of estrangement with courage and determination. Embrace challenges as opportunities for growth and learning, recognizing that adversity can foster inner strength and resilience. By reframing difficult situations as opportunities for personal development, you can shift your perspective and approach challenges with greater optimism and resilience.

FOCUS ON BUILDING COPING skills such as problem-solving, flexibility, and optimism. Develop strategies for effectively managing stress and adversity, such as breaking problems down into manageable steps, remaining adaptable in the face of change, and maintaining a positive outlook.

. . .

DRAW upon past experiences of resilience to remind yourself of your inner strength and capacity to overcome obstacles. Reflect on times when you have faced adversity and emerged stronger, using those experiences as inspiration and guidance. By recognizing your resilience, you can cultivate a sense of empowerment and confidence in navigating the challenges of estrangement with grace and grit.

BENEFITS OF RESILIENCE

1. **Increased Adaptability**: Resilience enhances adaptability, enabling individuals to navigate changes and setbacks easily.
2. **Improved Problem-Solving**: Building resilience fosters practical problem-solving skills, helping individuals address challenges constructively.
3. **Greater Optimism**: Resilience promotes a positive outlook, encouraging individuals to approach adversity with hope and confidence.
4. **Enhanced Self-Efficacy**: Cultivating resilience boosts self-efficacy, empowering individuals to believe in overcoming obstacles.

EXAMPLES OF CULTIVATING Resilience

. . .

EXAMPLE 1: Feeling overwhelmed by the challenges of estrangement from her partner, Lisa focuses on building her resilience. She practices problem-solving by breaking down her problems into manageable steps and remains flexible and adaptable in the face of change. This approach helps Lisa navigate her emotions and challenges more confidently and optimistically.

EXAMPLE 2: Tom, dealing with the stress of his father's estrangement, reflects on past experiences of resilience. He recalls times when he faced adversity and emerged stronger, using those experiences as inspiration and guidance. This practice helps Tom recognize his inner strength and approach his challenges with greater resilience and self-efficacy.

Seek Professional Help if Needed

IF YOU STRUGGLE to cope with the emotional toll of estrangement, don't hesitate to seek support from a therapist or counselor. Therapy can provide a safe and non-judgmental space to explore your feelings, gain insight into your coping mechanisms, and develop strategies for managing stress and anxiety.

. . .

BENEFITS of Professional Help

1. **Safe Space for Exploration**: Therapy offers a safe and supportive space for individuals to explore their emotions and experiences.
2. **Insight and Understanding**: Therapists provide valuable insights and understanding, helping individuals gain clarity and perspective on their challenges.
3. **Effective Coping Strategies**: Therapy helps individuals develop effective coping strategies for managing stress and adversity.
4. **Emotional Support**: Therapists offer emotional support and validation, helping individuals feel understood and accepted.

EXAMPLES OF SEEKING Professional Help

EXAMPLE 1: Emma, overwhelmed by the emotions surrounding her estrangement from her mother, decides to seek therapy. She finds a therapist specializing in family estrangement and begins regular sessions. Through treatment, Emma gains valuable insights into her emotions and develops effective coping strategies, helping her navigate her challenges with greater resilience and clarity.

. . .

EXAMPLE 2: David, struggling with anger and resentment due to his estrangement from his brother, seeks the support of a counselor. The counselor provides a safe space for David to explore his feelings and better understand his emotional responses. Through therapy, David develops healthier coping mechanisms and works towards healing and reconciliation.

∽

Self-Care Practices: Nurturing Your Mental, Emotional, and Physical Well-Being

SELF-CARE IS NOT JUST A LUXURY; it's a vital practice of intentional nurturing that prioritizes mental, emotional, and physical health, particularly during times of heightened stress and adversity. Amidst the tumultuous landscape of estrangement, self-care emerges as an indispensable lifeline, offering individuals a sanctuary of solace and renewal amid emotional upheaval and turmoil.

AT ITS ESSENCE, self-care is a radical act of self-love and self-compassion, inviting individuals to honor their intrinsic worth and prioritize their well-being above all else. It encompasses diverse practices and rituals, ranging from simple self-kindness to more elaborate self-indulgence, all aimed at nourishing the mind, body, and soul.

. . .

IN THE CONTEXT OF ESTRANGEMENT, self-care takes on heightened significance as individuals navigate the turbulent waters of fractured relationships and emotional discord. It becomes a cornerstone of resilience, offering individuals the tools and resources to weather the storms of estrangement with grace and grit.

MENTAL SELF-CARE INVOLVES NURTURING the mind through mindfulness meditation, cognitive-behavioral therapy, or engaging in activities that bring joy and fulfillment. By cultivating a mindful awareness of thoughts and emotions, individuals can navigate the complexities of estrangement with greater clarity and calmness, fostering a sense of inner peace and serenity amidst the chaos.

EMOTIONAL SELF-CARE ENTAILS TENDING to the heart and soul, acknowledging and honoring one's emotions with compassion and empathy. It may involve seeking support from trusted friends or loved ones, expressing emotions through creative outlets such as art or journaling, or engaging in activities that soothe and comfort the spirit. By embracing their feelings with courage and authenticity, individuals can cultivate emotional resilience and strength, enabling them to navigate the highs and lows of estrangement with greater ease and grace.

. . .

PHYSICAL SELF-CARE ENCOMPASSES practices that nurture the body and promote overall health and vitality. This may include regular exercise, eating nourishing foods, getting adequate rest and sleep, and prioritizing relaxation and rejuvenation. By caring for their physical well-being, individuals can bolster their resilience and vitality, fortifying themselves against the physical toll of stress and adversity.

SELF-CARE IS an essential practice for individuals navigating the complexities of estrangement. It offers a sanctuary of solace and renewal amidst the storms of emotional turmoil and discord. By prioritizing their mental, emotional, and physical health, individuals can cultivate resilience, manage stress, and promote overall well-being, empowering themselves to navigate the challenges of estrangement with grace, courage, and resilience.

BENEFITS OF SELF-CARE

1. **Improved Mental Health**: Self-care promotes mental health by reducing symptoms of anxiety and depression and fostering overall emotional well-being.
2. **Enhanced Physical Health**: Self-care practices such as regular exercise and adequate rest improve physical health, boosting energy levels and overall vitality.

3. **Greater Emotional Resilience**: Self-care fosters emotional resilience, helping individuals cope with stress and adversity more effectively.

4. **Increased Self-Awareness**: Self-care promotes self-awareness, allowing individuals to better understand their needs and emotions.

Examples of Self-Care Practices

Example 1: Feeling overwhelmed by the stress of her father's estrangement, Sarah prioritizes self-care by engaging in activities that bring her joy and relaxation. She spends time in nature, practices yoga, and indulges in her favorite hobbies. These practices help Sarah manage her stress and promote overall well-being.

Example 2: John, dealing with the emotional turmoil of estrangement from his partner, establishes a healthy routine that includes regular exercise, balanced meals, and adequate rest. He also engages in mindfulness meditation and journaling to process his emotions. These self-care practices help John cultivate resilience and navigate his challenges more easily.

Prioritize Self-Care Activities

PRIORITIZING self-care involves intentionally carving out time to engage in activities that nurture your mental, emotional, and physical well-being. This includes activities that bring you joy, relaxation, and fulfillment. Spending time in nature can be incredibly rejuvenating, offering a respite from the stresses of daily life and allowing you to reconnect with the natural world. Whether walking in the park, hiking, or simply sitting outside and soaking up the sunshine, immersing yourself in nature can help reduce stress and promote peace and tranquility.

PRACTICING a hobby is another essential aspect of self-care. Hobbies allow you to engage in enjoyable activities and create a sense of fulfillment. Whether painting, gardening, playing music, or any other activity that interests you, hobbies offer a valuable outlet for creativity and self-expression. Making time for hobbies can cultivate greater satisfaction and well-being in your life.

SIMILARLY, indulging in favorite pastimes is a beautiful way to prioritize self-care. Whether it's reading a book, watching a movie, or spending time with loved ones, engaging in activities that you find enjoyable and relaxing can help recharge your batteries and promote a sense of balance and contentment. Overall, prioritizing self-care activities is essential for maintaining a healthy and fulfilling lifestyle, allowing you to nurture your needs and cultivate a greater sense of well-being and resilience.

BENEFITS OF PRIORITIZING Self-Care Activities

1. **Reduced Stress**: Engaging in self-care activities helps reduce stress and promote relaxation.
2. **Increased Happiness**: Prioritizing activities that bring joy and fulfillment enhances happiness and well-being.
3. **Enhanced Creativity**: Engaging in hobbies and favorite pastimes fosters creativity and self-expression.
4. **Improved Life Balance**: Prioritizing self-care activities creates a healthier balance between personal needs and responsibilities.

EXAMPLES OF PRIORITIZING Self-Care Activities

EXAMPLE 1: Emma, feeling overwhelmed by the stress of estrangement from her sister, prioritizes self-care by spending time in nature. She takes daily walks in the park, finding solace and relaxation in the natural environment.

This practice helps Emma manage her stress and promote peace and tranquility.

EXAMPLE 2: David, struggling with the emotional turmoil of estrangement from his best friend, practices self-care by engaging in his favorite hobby, painting. He sets aside time each week to immerse himself in creative expression, which helps him process his emotions and find joy and fulfillment. This practice enhances David's overall well-being and fosters a sense of balance and contentment.

Establish Healthy Routines

HEALTHY ROUTINES SUPPORT your overall health and well-being. Maintaining a regular sleep schedule ensures your body gets the rest it needs to function optimally and promote mental clarity and emotional stability. Eating balanced meals gives your body the nutrients it needs to thrive, fueling your energy levels and supporting your immune system. Engaging in regular physical activity helps to strengthen your muscles and cardiovascular system, improve mood, and reduce stress. By incorporating these habits into your daily life, you can create a foundation of health and wellness that supports your overall well-being and resilience in the face of life's challenges.

. . .

BENEFITS OF HEALTHY **Routines**

1. **Improved Physical Health**: Healthy routines promote physical health, enhancing energy and overall vitality.
2. **Enhanced Mental Health**: Regular sleep, balanced meals, and physical activity improve mental health and emotional stability.
3. **Greater Resilience**: Healthy routines foster resilience, helping individuals cope with stress and adversity more effectively.
4. **Increased Productivity**: Establishing healthy routines enhances productivity and overall life balance.

∿

EXAMPLES OF HEALTHY **Routines**

EXAMPLE 1: Sarah, feeling overwhelmed by the stress of her father's estrangement, establishes a healthy routine that includes regular exercise, balanced meals, and adequate rest. She also practices mindfulness meditation and journaling to process her emotions. These healthy routines help Sarah cultivate resilience and navigate her challenges more easily.

. . .

EXAMPLE 2: When dealing with his partner's emotional turmoil of estrangement, John prioritizes self-care by engaging in activities that bring him joy and relaxation. He enjoys nature, practices yoga, and indulges in his favorite hobbies. These healthy routines help John manage his stress and promote overall well-being.

Engage in Activities Promoting Self-Expression

ENCOURAGING self-expression is a powerful way to process emotions and experiences. Through writing, art, music, or other creative outlets, you can externalize your inner thoughts and feelings, gaining insight into your emotional landscape and fostering a sense of clarity and understanding. Creative expression allows you to channel your emotions constructively, transforming pain into beauty and turmoil into inspiration. Creative expression offers a valuable outlet for self-discovery and healing, whether journaling to explore your thoughts, painting to capture your emotions visually, or playing music to express your innermost feelings. By engaging in activities that promote self-expression, you can cultivate a deeper connection to yourself and your experiences, empowering yourself to navigate life's challenges with resilience and grace.

BENEFITS OF SELF-EXPRESSION

1. **Emotional Release**: Engaging in self-expression provides an emotional release, helping individuals process and manage their emotions.
2. **Enhanced Self-Awareness**: Self-expression promotes self-awareness, allowing individuals to understand their thoughts and feelings better.
3. **Greater Creativity**: Engaging in creative activities fosters creativity and innovation.
4. **Improved Mental Health**: Self-expression reduces symptoms of anxiety and depression, promoting overall mental well-being.

EXAMPLES OF SELF-EXPRESSION

EXAMPLE 1: Emma, feeling overwhelmed by the emotions surrounding her estrangement from her mother, engages in self-expression through journaling. She writes about her thoughts and feelings daily, gaining valuable insights into her emotional landscape and fostering a sense of clarity and understanding. This practice helps Emma process her emotions and navigate challenges with greater resilience and grace.

EXAMPLE 2: David, struggling with anger and resentment due to his estrangement from his brother, engages in self-expression through painting. He visualizes his emotions, transforming his pain into beauty and inspiration. This practice provides an emotional release and fosters a deeper connection to himself and his experiences.

Setting Boundaries: Protecting Yourself and Managing Expectations

SETTING boundaries is a profound act of self-care and empowerment. It offers individuals a protective shield against emotional harm and a framework for navigating the complexities of estrangement with clarity and self-assurance. It involves establishing clear and firm limits with family members, friends, or others involved in the estrangement, delineating what behavior is acceptable and what is not, and asserting one's needs and boundaries in relationships.

ESTABLISHING clear boundaries begins with a deep understanding of one's own needs, values, and limits. It requires individuals to reflect on their emotional well-being and identify the behaviors or interactions that trigger or harm them. By acknowledging their needs and limits, individuals can gain clarity on what boundaries are necessary to protect themselves from emotional harm and maintain their self-respect and dignity.

. . .

ONCE INDIVIDUALS HAVE IDENTIFIED their boundaries, the next step is to communicate them clearly and assertively to those involved in the estrangement. This may include having difficult conversations with family members, friends, or others in which individuals express their boundaries clearly, respectfully, and non-confrontationally. Individuals must be firm and consistent in enforcing their limits, even in the face of resistance or pushback from others.

SETTING boundaries also involves being willing to enforce consequences when boundaries are violated. This may include taking a step back from the relationship, limiting contact with specific individuals, or seeking support from a therapist or counselor to process and cope with the emotional fallout of boundary violations. While enforcing boundaries can be challenging and uncomfortable, individuals must prioritize their emotional well-being and self-respect.

SETTING boundaries protects individuals from emotional harm and helps manage expectations in relationships. By clearly communicating their needs and limits, individuals can avoid misunderstandings and conflicts arising from unmet or unclear expectations. Setting boundaries allows individuals to define the terms of their relationships on their terms, fostering a sense of autonomy, agency, and empowerment.

ULTIMATELY, setting boundaries is a transformative act of self-love and self-advocacy. It empowers individuals to protect themselves from emotional harm, assert their needs and boundaries in relationships, and cultivate healthier, more respectful, and fulfilling connections with others. By establishing clear boundaries with family members, friends, or others involved in the estrangement, individuals can reclaim their sense of agency and sovereignty in the face of adversity, paving the way for healing, growth, and renewal.

BENEFITS OF SETTING Boundaries

1. **Emotional Protection**: Boundaries protect individuals from emotional harm, reducing the impact of negative interactions.
2. **Enhanced Self-Respect**: Setting boundaries fosters self-respect, reinforcing one's self-worth and dignity.
3. **Improved Relationships**: Boundaries create a foundation of mutual respect and understanding, fostering healthier and more balanced relationships.
4. **Greater Autonomy**: Establishing boundaries promotes autonomy, allowing individuals to

assert their needs and control their lives.

~

Examples of Setting Boundaries

Example 1: Sarah, feeling overwhelmed by her estrangement from her parents, sets clear boundaries regarding communication. She tells her parents she needs space and will only discuss their relationship once she feels ready. By asserting her needs, Sarah protects her emotional well-being and fosters a sense of self-respect.

Example 2: John, struggling with estrangement from his siblings, sets boundaries around family gatherings. He communicates that he will only attend events where respectful and constructive communication is prioritized. This boundary helps John navigate family interactions with greater clarity and self-assurance.

~

Identify Your Needs and Priorities

Identifying your needs and priorities in relationships is essential for maintaining emotional well-being and setting boundaries that align with your values. Take time to reflect on what matters most and where you may need to establish limits to safeguard your mental and emotional health. This could involve recognizing patterns of behavior or communication that leave you feeling drained or overwhelmed and taking steps to assert your boundaries in those areas. By clarifying your needs and priorities, you can cultivate healthier relationships built on mutual respect and understanding, creating space for personal growth and fulfillment.

BENEFITS OF IDENTIFYING **Needs and Priorities**

1. **Enhanced Self-Awareness**: Identifying needs and priorities fosters self-awareness, allowing individuals to understand their emotional landscape better.
2. **Improved Decision-Making**: Clarity on needs and priorities promotes informed and deliberate decision-making.
3. **Greater Emotional Well-Being**: Understanding and asserting one's needs supports emotional well-being and reduces stress.
4. **Increased Personal Growth**: Identifying needs and priorities encourages personal growth by fostering a deeper understanding of oneself.

EXAMPLES OF IDENTIFYING **Needs and Priorities**

. . .

Example 1: Emma, feeling overwhelmed by the stress of estrangement from her mother, takes time to reflect on her needs and priorities. She realizes that she needs space and time to process her emotions and sets boundaries around communication. This clarity helps Emma navigate her feelings and relationships with greater self-awareness and emotional well-being.

Example 2: David, struggling with his estrangement from his brother, identifies his need for respectful and constructive communication. He sets boundaries around family interactions, prioritizing environments that support positive communication. This practice fosters greater emotional well-being and promotes healthier relationships.

Communicate Clearly and Assertively

Communicating clearly and assertively is crucial for establishing and maintaining healthy relationship boundaries. By expressing your needs and preferences using "I" statements, you take ownership of your feelings and avoid blaming others. This approach fosters open and honest communication while promoting mutual understanding and respect. Be firm and consistent in enforcing your boundaries, and don't hesitate to assert yourself if they are crossed. Remember that setting boundaries is not about controlling others but advocating for your well-being and preserving your self-respect. Communicating assertively empowers you to create relationships built on mutual respect and understanding, where both parties feel heard, valued, and respected.

BENEFITS of Clear and Assertive Communication

1. **Improved Relationships**: Clear and assertive communication fosters healthier relationships built on mutual respect and understanding.
2. **Enhanced Self-Respect**: Assertive communication reinforces self-respect and self-worth.
3. **Greater Emotional Clarity**: Clear communication promotes emotional clarity, reducing misunderstandings and conflicts.
4. **Increased Confidence**: Assertive communication boosts confidence, empowering individuals to assert their needs and boundaries.

EXAMPLES of Clear and Assertive Communication

. . .

Example 1: Feeling overwhelmed by her estrangement from her parents, Sarah communicates her boundaries clearly and assertively. She uses "I" statements to express her need for space and explains that she will not discuss their relationship until she feels ready. This approach fosters open and honest communication and promotes mutual understanding.

Example 2: John, struggling with his estrangement from his siblings, communicates his boundaries around family gatherings clearly and assertively. He expresses his need for respectful and constructive communication and explains that he will only attend events where this is prioritized. This practice promotes emotional clarity and fosters healthier family interactions.

Be Flexible and Adaptable

Being flexible and adaptable to boundaries is essential for navigating relationships and personal growth complexities. Recognize that boundaries are not fixed entities but somewhat fluid guidelines that may need to evolve to accommodate shifting needs and circumstances. Stay attuned to changes in your life, such as transitions, new experiences, or shifts in priorities, and be willing to adjust your boundaries accordingly. This may involve renegotiating agreements with others, setting new limits, or revisiting existing boundaries to ensure they align with your values and well-being. By remaining flexible and open to change, you empower yourself to navigate life's twists and turns with resilience and grace, fostering healthy relationships and personal growth.

BENEFITS OF FLEXIBILITY **and Adaptability**

1. **Increased Resilience**: Flexibility and adaptability foster resilience, helping individuals navigate changes and setbacks more effectively.
2. **Improved Relationships**: Adaptable boundaries promote healthier and more balanced relationships.
3. **Greater Emotional Stability**: Flexibility supports emotional stability by allowing individuals to adjust their boundaries as needed.
4. **Enhanced Personal Growth**: Adaptable boundaries encourage personal growth by accommodating evolving needs and circumstances.

EXAMPLES OF FLEXIBILITY **and Adaptability**

EXAMPLE 1: Emma, feeling overwhelmed by the stress of estrangement from her mother, remains flexible and adaptable in her boundaries. She recognizes that her needs may change and is willing to adjust her boundaries accordingly. This approach fosters resilience and emotional stability.

EXAMPLE 2: David, struggling with his estrangement from his brother, practices flexibility and adaptability in his boundaries. He stays attuned to changes in his life and relationships and will renegotiate agreements as needed. This practice promotes healthier relationships and personal growth.

Respect Others' Boundaries

RESPECTING the boundaries of others involved in the estrangement is crucial for fostering trust, mutual respect, and healthy communication. It's essential to acknowledge and honor the limits that others have set for themselves, even if they differ from your preferences or desires. Avoid crossing or pressuring them to change their boundaries to suit your needs, as this can erode trust and create conflict. Instead, demonstrate empathy and understanding by validating their feelings and choices, even if you may not fully agree with them. By respecting the boundaries of others, you create a safe and supportive environment where everyone feels valued, heard, and respected, fostering healthier relationships and promoting mutual healing and reconciliation.

. . .

Benefits of Respecting Others' Boundaries

1. **Enhanced Trust**: Respecting others' boundaries fosters trust and mutual respect in relationships.
2. **Improved Communication**: Acknowledging and honoring others' limits promotes healthier and more effective communication.
3. **Greater Emotional Safety**: Respecting boundaries creates a sense of emotional safety and stability in relationships.
4. **Increased Relationship Satisfaction**: Honoring others' boundaries fosters more balanced and fulfilling relationships.

Examples of Respecting Others' Boundaries

EXAMPLE 1: Sarah, feeling overwhelmed by her estrangement from her parents, respects her parents' boundaries by acknowledging their need for space and time to process their emotions. She avoids pressuring them to change their limits and demonstrates empathy and understanding. This approach fosters trust and mutual respect.

. . .

EXAMPLE 2: John, struggling with estrangement from his siblings, respects his siblings' boundaries by honoring their preferences and limits. He avoids crossing their boundaries or pressuring them to change and demonstrates empathy and understanding. This practice promotes healthier family interactions and emotional safety.

∼

Setting Boundaries: Advanced Strategies and Considerations

SETTING boundaries is not a one-size-fits-all approach; it requires nuance, awareness, and ongoing evaluation. Here, we delve deeper into more advanced strategies and considerations to help individuals navigate this complex process effectively.

UNDERSTAND the Types of Boundaries

Boundaries can be categorized into different types, each serving a unique relationship purpose. These include:

- **Emotional Boundaries**: These protect your emotional well-being by limiting how much emotional energy you invest in a relationship. Emotional boundaries help prevent emotional exhaustion and protect against emotional manipulation or abuse.

- **Physical Boundaries**: These pertain to personal space and physical touch. They ensure that you feel safe and respected in your physical interactions with others.
- **Mental Boundaries**: These involve your thoughts, values, and opinions. They protect your right to think independently and prevent others from imposing their beliefs on you.
- **Time Boundaries**: These help you manage your time effectively, ensuring you have enough time for yourself and your responsibilities. They prevent others from monopolizing your time and help you maintain a healthy work-life balance.
- **Material Boundaries**: These protect your personal belongings and financial resources. Material boundaries ensure that others respect your possessions and economic limits.

Understanding the different types of boundaries can help you identify where to set limits in your relationships. Recognizing and establishing these boundaries can create a more balanced and respectful dynamic with others.

BENEFITS OF UNDERSTANDING the Types of Boundaries

1. **Improved Emotional Health**: Emotional boundaries protect against emotional exhaustion and manipulation, promoting overall emotional

health.

2. **Enhanced Physical Safety**: Physical boundaries ensure safety and respect in physical interactions.

3. **Greater Intellectual Autonomy**: Mental boundaries foster intellectual autonomy and protect against unwanted influence.

4. **Increased Time Management**: Time boundaries support effective time management and work-life balance.

5. **Protected Personal Resources**: Material boundaries safeguard personal belongings and financial resources.

EXAMPLES OF UNDERSTANDING **the Types of Boundaries**

Example 1: Feeling overwhelmed by her estrangement from her parents, Sarah sets emotional boundaries by limiting the emotional energy she invests in the relationship. She ensures she has enough time and space to prioritize her emotional well-being, promoting overall emotional health.

EXAMPLE 2: John, struggling with his estrangement from his siblings, establishes time boundaries by managing his time effectively and ensuring he has enough time for himself and his responsibilities. This practice supports work-life balance and promotes a healthier dynamic in his relationships.

. . .

Use Technology to Reinforce Boundaries

In today's digital age, technology can be a valuable tool for reinforcing boundaries. Here are some ways to use technology effectively:

- **Communication Filters**: Use features like call blocking, email filters, and social media privacy settings to limit unwanted contact. This can help you maintain your boundaries and reduce stress from constant communication.
- **Scheduled Responses**: Set specific times to respond to messages and emails rather than feeling pressured to reply immediately. This helps you manage your time better and prevents others from infringing on your time.
- **Digital Detox**: Regularly disconnect from digital devices to recharge and focus on self-care. This can help you maintain a healthy balance between your digital and personal life.

Using technology mindfully reinforces your boundaries and creates a healthier balance in your interactions.

Benefits of Using Technology to Reinforce Boundaries

1. **Reduced Stress**: Technology features like call blocking and email filters reduce stress by limiting unwanted contact.
2. **Improved Time Management**: Scheduled responses and digital detoxes support effective time management and balance.
3. **Enhanced Privacy**: Privacy settings on social media platforms protect personal information and interactions.
4. **Increased Digital Well-Being**: Regularly disconnecting from digital devices promotes overall digital well-being.

EXAMPLES OF USING Technology to Reinforce Boundaries

EXAMPLE 1: Emma, feeling overwhelmed by the stress of estrangement from her mother, uses technology to reinforce her boundaries. She sets specific times to respond to messages and emails and regularly disconnects from digital devices to focus on self-care. This practice promotes a healthier balance between her digital and personal life.

EXAMPLE 2: David, struggling with his estrangement from his brother, uses communication filters to limit unwanted contact. He sets privacy settings on social media platforms to protect his personal information and interactions. This practice helps David maintain his boundaries and reduce stress.

Practice Boundary Affirmations

AFFIRMATIONS ARE positive statements that reinforce your beliefs and intentions. Practicing boundary affirmations can help you internalize your commitment to setting and maintaining boundaries. Here are some examples:

- "I have the right to set boundaries that protect my well-being."
- "I am worthy of respect and consideration in all my relationships."
- "Setting boundaries is an act of self-love and self-respect."
- "I can say no without feeling guilty or ashamed."

Repeat these affirmations regularly to strengthen your resolve and confidence in setting boundaries.

BENEFITS of Boundary Affirmations

1. **Increased Confidence**: Affirmations boost confidence and reinforce the commitment to setting boundaries.

2. **Enhanced Self-Respect**: Affirmations promote self-respect and self-worth.

3. **Improved Emotional Health**: Positive affirmations support overall emotional health and well-being.

4. **Greater Clarity**: Affirmations provide clarity and focus on setting and maintaining boundaries.

EXAMPLES of Boundary Affirmations

EXAMPLE 1: Feeling overwhelmed by her estrangement from her parents, Sarah regularly practices boundary affirmations. She repeats statements like "I have the right to set boundaries that protect my well-being" and "I am worthy of respect and consideration in all my relationships." These affirmations boost Sarah's confidence and reinforce her commitment to setting boundaries.

EXAMPLE 2: John, struggling with estrangement from his siblings, uses boundary affirmations to strengthen his resolve. He repeats statements like "Setting boundaries is an act of self-love and self-respect" and "I can say no without feeling guilty or ashamed." These affirmations promote self-respect and support John's emotional health.

Develop Conflict Resolution Skills

SETTING boundaries can sometimes lead to conflicts, especially if others resist or challenge your limits. Developing conflict resolution skills can help you navigate these situations more effectively. Key skills include:

- **Active Listening**: Show empathy and understanding by listening to the other person's perspective without interrupting. This can help de-escalate tensions and foster mutual respect.
- **Assertive Communication**: Express your needs and boundaries clearly and respectfully without being aggressive or confrontational. Use "I" statements to take ownership of your feelings and avoid blaming others.
- **Compromise and Negotiation**: Be willing to find common ground and work towards mutually acceptable solutions. This can help maintain positive relationships while respecting your boundaries.
- **Emotional Regulation**: Manage your emotions effectively during conflicts to stay calm and composed. Practice techniques like deep breathing, mindfulness, and self-soothing to maintain emotional control.

By honing these skills, you can handle boundary-related conflicts constructively and maintain healthier relationships.

Benefits of Conflict Resolution Skills

1. **Improved Relationships**: Effective conflict resolution skills promote healthier and more balanced relationships.
2. **Enhanced Emotional Control**: Conflict resolution skills support emotional regulation and stability.
3. **Greater Mutual Respect**: Active listening and assertive communication foster mutual respect and understanding.
4. **Increased Problem-Solving**: Compromise and negotiation promote effective problem-solving and collaboration.

Examples of Conflict Resolution Skills

Example 1: Emma, feeling overwhelmed by the stress of estrangement from her mother, develops conflict resolution skills to navigate boundary-related conflicts. She practices active listening, assertive communication, and emotional regulation, which help her handle conflicts constructively and maintain healthier relationships.

EXAMPLE 2: David, struggling with estrangement from his brother, hones his conflict resolution skills by focusing on compromise and negotiation. He remains open to finding common ground and works towards mutually acceptable solutions. This practice promotes effective problem-solving and fosters mutual respect in his relationships.

Seek Support for Boundary Challenges

SETTING and maintaining boundaries can be challenging, especially in deeply entrenched or emotionally charged relationships. Seeking support from a therapist, counselor, or support group can provide valuable guidance and encouragement. These professionals can help you:

- Identify and understand your boundary needs
- Develop effective communication strategies
- Process and cope with the emotional impact of setting boundaries
- Build confidence and resilience in maintaining your limits

Support from others who understand your struggles can also provide a sense of validation and empowerment, helping you stay committed to your boundary-setting journey.

Benefits of Seeking Support for Boundary Challenges

1. **Emotional Validation**: Support from therapists, counselors, or support groups provides emotional validation and understanding.
2. **Improved Communication**: Professional support helps individuals develop effective communication strategies.
3. **Enhanced Confidence**: Support fosters confidence and resilience in setting and maintaining boundaries.
4. **Greater Emotional Well-Being**: Seeking support promotes overall emotional well-being and reduces stress.

EXAMPLES OF SEEKING SUPPORT FOR BOUNDARY CHALLENGES

Example 1: Feeling overwhelmed by her estrangement from her parents, Sarah seeks support from a therapist to navigate boundary challenges. The therapist provides valuable guidance and helps Sarah develop effective communication strategies, fostering confidence and resilience in maintaining her boundaries.

. . .

EXAMPLE **2**: John, struggling with his estrangement from his siblings, joins a support group to seek validation and encouragement for his boundary-setting journey. The support group offers understanding and empowerment, helping John stay committed to his boundaries and promoting his emotional well-being.

Integrating Boundaries into Daily Life

INTEGRATING boundaries into your daily life involves consistent practice and self-awareness. Here are some practical tips for maintaining boundaries in various aspects of your life:

PERSONAL RELATIONSHIPS

In personal relationships, boundaries help create a balanced and respectful dynamic. Here are some ways to integrate boundaries into your personal life:

- **Communicate Expectations**: Clearly express your expectations and limits to family members and friends. This can prevent misunderstandings and ensure everyone is on the same page.
- **Limit Access**: Decide who can access your time,

space, and resources. This can involve limiting visits, phone calls, or financial support to maintain your well-being.

- **Prioritize Self-Care**: Make self-care a non-negotiable part of your routine. This can include setting aside time for relaxation, hobbies, and personal growth activities.

BENEFITS OF INTEGRATING **Boundaries in Personal Relationships**

1. **Improved Relationship Dynamics**: Clear boundaries create balanced and respectful relationships.
2. **Enhanced Emotional Health**: Boundaries support emotional health and reduce stress.
3. **Greater Personal Growth**: Prioritizing self-care fosters personal growth and well-being.
4. **Increased Clarity and Understanding**: Communicating expectations prevents misunderstandings and promotes mutual understanding.

EXAMPLES OF INTEGRATING **Boundaries in Personal Relationships**

. . .

EXAMPLE 1: Emma, feeling overwhelmed by the stress of estrangement from her mother, integrates boundaries into her relationships by clearly expressing her expectations and limits. She communicates her needs to family members and friends, ensuring everyone is on the same page and fostering balanced and respectful relationships.

EXAMPLE 2: David, struggling with his estrangement from his brother, limits access to his time and resources. He decides who can access his time and space and prioritizes self-care by setting aside time for relaxation and hobbies. This practice supports David's emotional health and promotes personal growth.

PROFESSIONAL RELATIONSHIPS

In professional settings, boundaries help maintain a healthy work-life balance and prevent burnout. Here are some tips for setting boundaries at work:

- **Set Work Hours**: Clearly define your work hours and stick to them. Avoid answering work-related calls or emails outside these hours to maintain a healthy balance.
- **Delegate Tasks**: Delegate tasks when necessary to avoid overloading yourself. This can help you

manage your workload more effectively and reduce stress.

- **Communicate Limits**: Communicate your limits to colleagues and supervisors. Let them know when you are unavailable, or a task exceeds your capacity.

BENEFITS OF SETTING Boundaries in Professional Relationships

1. **Improved Work-Life Balance**: Clear boundaries support a healthy balance between work and personal life.
2. **Enhanced Productivity**: Effective delegation and communication promote productivity and reduce stress.
3. **Greater Emotional Well-Being**: Boundaries prevent burnout and support overall emotional well-being.
4. **Increased Professional Respect**: Communicating limits fosters mutual respect and understanding in professional settings.

～

EXAMPLES OF SETTING Boundaries in Professional Relationships

. . .

EXAMPLE 1: Feeling overwhelmed by her estrangement from her parents, Sarah sets precise work hours and sticks to them. She avoids answering work-related calls or emails outside these hours, maintaining a healthy balance between work and personal life. This practice supports her emotional well-being and promotes productivity.

EXAMPLE 2: John, struggling with his estrangement from his siblings, delegates tasks at work to avoid overloading himself. He communicates his limits to colleagues and supervisors, ensuring they know when he is unavailable or a task exceeds his capacity. This practice promotes a healthier work-life balance and fosters professional respect.

Social Media and Digital Spaces

SETTING boundaries in social media and online interactions is essential in the digital age. Here are some ways to protect your digital well-being:

- **Manage Privacy Settings**: Adjust your privacy settings on social media platforms to control who can see your posts and interact with you.
- **Limit Screen Time**: Set limits on your screen time

to prevent digital overload. Use apps or built-in device features to monitor and manage your usage.

- **Curate Your Feed**: Curate your social media feed to include content that uplifts and inspires you. Unfollow or mute accounts that cause stress or negativity.

BENEFITS OF SETTING Boundaries in Social Media and Digital Spaces

1. **Enhanced Digital Well-Being**: Boundaries support overall digital well-being and prevent digital overload.
2. **Improved Privacy**: Privacy settings protect personal information and interactions.
3. **Greater Emotional Health**: Curating your social media feed promotes emotional health and reduces stress.
4. **Increased Focus and Productivity**: Limiting screen time supports focus and productivity.

∿

EXAMPLES OF SETTING Boundaries in Social Media and Digital Spaces

. . .

EXAMPLE 1: Emma, feeling overwhelmed by the stress of estrangement from her mother, sets boundaries in her social media interactions. She adjusts her privacy settings to control who can see her posts and interact with her, promoting digital well-being and protecting her personal information.

EXAMPLE 2: David, struggling with his estrangement from his brother, limits his screen time to prevent digital overload. He uses apps to monitor and manage his usage and curates his social media feed to include content that uplifts and inspires him. This practice promotes emotional health and reduces stress.

The Long-Term Benefits of Boundaries

ESTABLISHING and maintaining boundaries offers numerous long-term benefits, contributing to well-being and healthier relationships. Here are some key benefits:

IMPROVED SELF-ESTEEM

Setting boundaries enhances self-esteem by reinforcing one's sense of self-worth and self-respect. When one prioritizes one's needs and asserts one's limits, one sends a powerful message to oneself and others that one deserves to be treated with dignity and respect.

. . .

Enhanced Relationships

Boundaries create a foundation of mutual respect and understanding in relationships. You foster healthier and more balanced connections with others by clearly communicating your needs and limits. This can lead to deeper, more fulfilling relationships built on trust and respect.

Reduced Stress and Burnout

Boundaries help manage stress and prevent burnout by ensuring you have enough time and energy for yourself. By limiting your time and responsibilities, you can avoid over-committing and create a more balanced and sustainable lifestyle.

Greater Emotional Stability

Boundaries contribute to excellent emotional stability by protecting you from emotional harm and reducing the impact of negative interactions. Maintaining clear and consistent boundaries can create a sense of emotional safety and stability.

Coping with Resistance to Boundaries

Setting boundaries can sometimes lead to resistance from others, mainly if they are not accustomed to respecting your limits. Here are some strategies for coping with resistance:

Stay Firm and Consistent

Staying firm and consistent in enforcing your boundaries is crucial for maintaining their effectiveness. Even if others resist or push back, it's important to remain steadfast in your commitment to your well-being. Consistency reinforces your boundaries and communicates that they are non-negotiable.

Use Positive Reinforcement

Use positive reinforcement to encourage others to respect your boundaries. Acknowledge and appreciate when others honor your limits, and express gratitude for their understanding. Positive reinforcement can create a more cooperative and respectful dynamic.

Seek Mediation or Support

If resistance to your boundaries leads to significant conflict, consider seeking mediation or support from a neutral third party, such as a therapist or counselor. Mediation can facilitate constructive dialogue and find mutually acceptable solutions.

Reevaluate Relationships

Sometimes, persistent resistance to your boundaries may indicate a need to reevaluate the relationship. Assess whether the relationship is healthy and supportive and aligns with your values and well-being. Sometimes, stepping away from toxic or harmful relationships is necessary for your emotional health.

BENEFITS OF COPING with Resistance to Boundaries

1. **Enhanced Boundary Effectiveness**: Staying firm and consistent reinforces the effectiveness of boundaries.
2. **Improved Relationship Dynamics**: Positive reinforcement fosters a more cooperative and respectful dynamic.
3. **More excellent Conflict Resolution**: Mediation and support facilitate constructive conflict resolution.
4. **Increased Emotional Well-Being**: Reevaluating relationships supports emotional health and reduces stress.

∽

EXAMPLES OF COPING with Resistance to Boundaries

. . .

EXAMPLE 1: Emma, feeling overwhelmed by the stress of estrangement from her mother, copes with resistance to her boundaries by staying firm and consistent. She uses positive reinforcement to encourage her mother to respect her limits and seeks mediation from a therapist to facilitate constructive dialogue. This approach enhances the effectiveness of her boundaries and promotes emotional well-being.

EXAMPLE 2: David, struggling with his estrangement from his brother, copes with resistance to his boundaries by seeking support from a counselor. The counselor helps David navigate conflicts and find mutually acceptable solutions. David also reevaluates his relationship with his brother, assessing whether it aligns with his values and well-being. This practice supports David's emotional health and fosters healthier relationships.

Embracing Boundaries as a Path to Empowerment

SETTING boundaries is a transformative journey of self-discovery, self-respect, and empowerment. It involves understanding your needs and limits, communicating them clearly and assertively, and maintaining them consistently. Boundaries protect your emotional well-being, foster healthier relationships, and create a foundation for personal growth and fulfillment.

. . .

As YOU NAVIGATE the complexities of estrangement and relationships, remember that setting boundaries is an act of self-love and self-advocacy. Embrace this journey with courage, resilience, and compassion, and know that prioritizing your well-being creates a healthier, more balanced, and fulfilling life.

By INTEGRATING the strategies and insights shared in this chapter, you can develop the skills and confidence to set and maintain boundaries that support your well-being and empower you to navigate the challenges of estrangement with grace and strength.

CHAPTER 3
BOOK REVIEW REQUEST

~

Make a Difference with Your Review

Unlock the Power of Generosity

=====================================

"Sometimes the most ordinary things could be made extraordinary, simply by doing them with the right people." – Nicholas Sparks.

=================================

. . .

DEAR READER,

Thank you for taking the time to read "Estranged Relationships" by Michael Stevens. We hope you found the book insightful and thought-provoking. Your opinion matters greatly to us and future readers seeking understanding and comfort in their journeys with estrangement.

Why Your Review Matters

YOUR REVIEW CAN MAKE a significant difference. By sharing your thoughts and experiences with this book, you can help others decide if it's the proper read for them. Your insights might be the guiding light someone needs to navigate their complex relationships.

What to Include in Your Review

- **Your Overall Impression:** What did you think about the book? Did it meet your expectations?
- **Key Takeaways:** What are your main points or lessons from the book? How did it impact your understanding of estrangement?
- **Personal Connection:** Did any part of the book resonate with your experiences? How?
- **Recommendations:** Would you recommend this book to others? If so, why and to whom?

. . .

How to Leave a Review

LEAVING a review is simple and quick:

- **eBook Readers: Click on the Link -** https://www.
  amazon.com/review/create-review/edit?channel=
  glance-detail&ie=UTF8&asin=B0D34NQFS9

- **Paperback, Hardcover, or iPads:** Scan the QR
  Code -

- **Click on "Write a Review".**
- **Share your thoughts and give a rating.**

. . .

Spread the Word

FEEL free to share your review on social media or with friends and family who might benefit from reading "Estranged Relationships." Your recommendation can help others discover the book and gain the support they need.

THANK you again for your support and for being part of our community. Your review can make a meaningful impact.

WARM REGARDS,

MICHAEL Stevens

CHAPTER 4

SEEKING SUPPORT AND GUIDANCE

⁓

In times of estrangement, individuals often find themselves grappling with a myriad of complex emotions and uncertainties. The rupture of family bonds and the strain on relationships can leave individuals feeling isolated, overwhelmed, and unsure of how to navigate the challenging road ahead. In these moments of turmoil, seeking support and guidance becomes essential for finding a sense of direction, healing, and hope.

PROFESSIONAL THERAPY and support groups offer valuable avenues for navigating estrangement's complexities. Therapists and counselors provide a safe and supportive space for individuals to explore their emotions, process their experiences, and develop coping strategies for managing the challenges of estrangement. Support groups offer the opportunity to connect with others facing similar struggles, providing solidarity, understanding, and shared experiences.

HOWEVER, spiritual resources provide comfort, solace, and resilience in estrangement for many individuals. Spirituality encompasses many beliefs, practices, and traditions that offer guidance, meaning, and connection to something greater than oneself. Whether rooted in organized religion, personal beliefs, or spiritual practices, spirituality provides a framework for understanding the deeper meaning behind life's challenges and finding strength in times of adversity.

AT THE HEART of spirituality lies the belief in a higher power or divine presence that offers love, compassion, and guidance to those who seek it. Individuals often turn to prayer, meditation, scripture, or other spiritual practices to connect with this higher power and find comfort in times of distress. Through prayer, individuals express their deepest hopes, fears, and longings, finding reassurance that they are not alone in their struggles.

MEDITATION OFFERS a pathway to inner peace and clarity, allowing individuals to quiet the mind, cultivate mindfulness, and access a sense of calm amidst the chaos of estrangement. Scripture and spiritual teachings provide timeless wisdom, offering insights into forgiveness, compassion, and resilience that can guide individuals through the challenges of estrangement.

FAITH-BASED communities also play a significant role in supporting and guiding individuals experiencing estrangement. Churches, mosques, temples, and synagogues serve as sanctuaries of compassion, understanding, and fellowship, where individuals can find solace in their fellow believers' shared faith and camaraderie. Spiritual leaders, clergy members, and fellow congregants offer counsel, prayers, and practical assistance to those in need, strengthening and encouraging their journey of healing and reconciliation.

IN INTEGRATING spirituality into their healing journey, individuals find a sense of purpose, meaning, and resilience that transcends the challenges of estrangement. By cultivating their spiritual connection and drawing upon the resources of their faith tradition, individuals can navigate the complexities of estrangement with grace, courage, and hope. In times of darkness, spirituality serves as a guiding light, illuminating the path forward and offering comfort and solace.

Spiritual Resources: Finding Comfort and Guidance

WITH ITS UPHEAVAL of familial bonds and emotional turmoil, estrangement often leads individuals on a profound inner journey of existential questioning and soul-searching. In these moments of inner turbulence, spiritual beliefs and practices emerge as invaluable sources of solace, offering a sense of purpose, meaning, and connection to something greater than oneself. Through prayer, meditation, scripture study, or contemplative reflection, individuals find refuge and guidance in turning to their spiritual traditions to navigate the complexities of estrangement.

AT THE CORE of spiritual practice lies the act of prayer, a sacred dialogue between the individual and a Higher Power. In the quiet sanctuary of worship, individuals lay bare their deepest fears, hopes, and longings, seeking solace and guidance in the belief that they are not alone in their struggles. Through prayer, individuals cultivate a sense of intimacy and connection with the divine, finding comfort in the knowledge that they are held in the loving embrace of a compassionate and understanding Creator.

MEDITATION IS another potent tool for navigating the challenges of estrangement, offering a pathway to inner peace and clarity amidst the storm of emotions. Through meditation, individuals learn to still the constant chatter of the mind, cultivate mindfulness, and access a place of calm and serenity within themselves. In meditation, individuals discover a reservoir of strength and resilience, tapping into the wellspring of inner wisdom that lies dormant.

SCRIPTURE STUDY and contemplative reflection provide additional avenues for finding comfort and guidance in estrangement. Sacred texts and teachings offer timeless wisdom and insight into the human condition, illuminating paths of forgiveness, compassion, and healing. Through the study of scripture, individuals draw inspiration from the lives of spiritual exemplars who have faced adversity with grace and grit, finding solace in their stories of resilience and redemption.

IN ADDITION to these personal practices, individuals often find support and camaraderie within their faith communities. Churches, mosques, temples, and synagogues serve as sanctuaries of compassion, understanding, and fellowship, where individuals can find solace in their fellow believers' shared faith and camaraderie. Spiritual leaders, clergy members, and fellow congregants offer counsel, prayers, and practical assistance to those in need, strengthening and encouraging their journey of healing and reconciliation.

. . .

Moreover, spiritual traditions offer a broader framework for understanding and making sense of the challenges of estrangement. They provide a lens through which individuals can view their experiences in the context of a larger cosmic narrative, finding meaning and purpose amid adversity. By anchoring themselves in their spiritual beliefs and practices, individuals can transcend the limitations of their circumstances and connect with a more profound sense of meaning and significance.

Spiritual resources serve as invaluable sources of comfort, guidance, and resilience for individuals navigating the complexities of estrangement. Whether through prayer, meditation, scripture study, or participation in faith communities, individuals find solace in turning to their spiritual traditions to find meaning and purpose amidst the challenges of estrangement. In spiritual practice, individuals discover a profound connection to something greater than themselves, finding strength and resilience to navigate the turbulent waters of estrangement with grace and courage.

Community Connections: Seeking Support in Faith-Based Communities

Estrangement, with its intricate web of emotional turmoil and relational fractures, often prompts individuals to seek solace and support within the embrace of their faith-based communities. Whether in churches, mosques, temples, or synagogues, these sacred spaces serve as sanctuaries of compassion, understanding, and empathy for individuals grappling with the complexities of family discord. Within the supportive embrace of their faith communities, individuals find strength, resilience, and hope as they navigate the turbulent waters of estrangement.

AT THE HEART of these faith-based communities are spiritual leaders, clergy members, and fellow believers who serve as guides, mentors, and companions on the journey of estrangement. Through their compassionate presence, empathetic listening, and wise counsel, these spiritual mentors offer light amidst the darkness of emotional turmoil and relational strife. Whether through pastoral counseling sessions, support groups, or informal conversations over coffee, individuals find solace in the shared fellowship of those who understand the challenges of estrangement and offer a compassionate ear and a comforting presence.

GROUP PRAYERS and worship services provide sacred spaces for individuals to unite in solidarity, offering their collective prayers and intentions for healing, reconciliation, and restoration. Amid these communal gatherings, individuals find strength in their fellow believers' shared faith and camaraderie, knowing they are not alone in their struggles.

Through the power of communal prayer, individuals draw upon the collective energy and spiritual support of their faith community, finding comfort and reassurance in the knowledge that they are held in the loving embrace of a compassionate and understanding Higher Power.

SUPPORT CIRCLES and small group discussions offer additional avenues for individuals to share their stories, express their emotions, and receive peer support and encouragement. Within these intimate settings, individuals find a safe space to open up about their struggles, fears, and hopes, knowing they will be met with empathy, understanding, and acceptance. Through the power of shared vulnerability and authentic connection, individuals experience a profound sense of belonging and validation, knowing they are valued and supported by their faith community.

MOREOVER, faith-based communities offer practical assistance and resources to needy individuals, providing a lifeline of support during times of crisis and uncertainty. Whether through benevolent funds, food pantries, or volunteer networks, faith communities extend a helping hand to those facing financial hardship, housing instability, or other material needs. Through these acts of kindness and generosity, individuals find tangible expressions of love and support from their faith community, knowing they are cared for and valued as cherished community members.

. . .

FAITH-BASED communities serve as vital sources of support, comfort, and guidance for individuals navigating the challenges of estrangement. Through the compassionate presence of spiritual leaders, the shared fellowship of fellow believers, and the power of communal prayer and worship, individuals find strength, resilience, and hope as they journey through the tumultuous terrain of estrangement. In the embrace of their faith community, individuals find solace in the knowledge that they are not alone in their struggles. Instead, they are surrounded by a supportive network of caring and compassionate individuals who walk alongside them toward healing and reconciliation.

Integrating Spirituality into Healing Practices

THE JOURNEY of healing and reconciliation following estrangement is not merely physical or emotional; it is also deeply spiritual. Integrating spirituality into healing practices provides individuals with a profound framework for understanding and navigating the complexities of estrangement. Through principles of forgiveness, reconciliation, and grace, individuals embark on a transformative journey of inner growth and renewal.

FORGIVENESS

Forgiveness is a profound concept that lies at the core of spiritual healing. It embodies relinquishing resentment and anger toward those who have caused pain or harm. However, forgiveness from a spiritual perspective transcends mere pardon; it is a transformative process of liberation and renewal.

FROM A SPIRITUAL VIEWPOINT, forgiveness is not about condoning or excusing the actions of others. Instead, it is about liberating oneself from the burden of carrying grudges and resentments. When individuals hold onto anger and resentment, it weighs heavily on their hearts and souls, hindering their ability to experience inner peace and fulfillment. By embracing forgiveness, individuals release themselves from the shackles of the past, allowing them to move forward with a lighter heart and a clearer mind.

FORGIVENESS IS AN EMPOWERING act that enables individuals to reclaim their power and agency. Rather than being bound by past hurts, forgiveness empowers individuals to control their emotional well-being. It is a conscious choice to let go of negative emotions and embrace the present moment with compassion and grace. Through forgiveness, individuals recognize that holding onto anger and resentment only perpetuates their suffering, while letting go allows them to experience freedom and inner peace.

MOREOVER, forgiveness is a profoundly transformative process that fosters personal growth and spiritual evolution. It requires individuals to confront their pain and vulnerability and acknowledge the humanity of themselves and those who have wronged them. In doing so, individuals cultivate empathy and compassion, recognizing the shared humanity that binds us together. Through forgiveness, individuals transcend the cycle of hurt and retaliation, choosing instead to respond with love and understanding.

IN ESSENCE, forgiveness is a journey of self-discovery and self-compassion. It requires individuals to look within themselves, confront their demons, and find the strength to let go of past grievances. Forgiveness is a testament to the resilience of the human spirit, demonstrating the capacity for growth, healing, and transformation. Through forgiveness, individuals free themselves from the chains of the past but also open themselves up to the possibility of a brighter, more fulfilling future.

FORGIVENESS IS a powerful act of liberation and renewal at the heart of spiritual healing. It is a conscious choice to release resentment and anger towards those who have caused pain or harm, freeing oneself from grudges and resentments. Through forgiveness, individuals reclaim their power and agency, embracing the present moment with compassion and grace.

RECONCILIATION

Reconciliation is a profound process at the heart of spiritual healing. It entails restoring broken relationships and rebuilding trust and connection with estranged loved ones. Unlike forgiveness, which can be solitary, reconciliation involves mutual engagement and dialogue between estranged parties. It requires humility, empathy, and a genuine desire to bridge the divide that separates them.

FROM A SPIRITUAL PERSPECTIVE, reconciliation is viewed as a sacred journey of healing and transformation. It is guided by love, compassion, and understanding principles and aims to restore harmony and unity within relationships. Reconciliation is not about sweeping past grievances under the rug or pretending that hurtful actions did not occur. Instead, it is about facing the truth of what has transpired, acknowledging the pain and suffering that both parties have experienced, and seeking a path forward together.

CENTRAL to the reconciliation process is the practice of empathy—the ability to understand and share another person's feelings. Empathy allows individuals to step into the shoes of their estranged loved ones, see the world from their perspective, and recognize the validity of their emotions and experiences. Through empathy, estranged parties can find common ground, bridge the gap of misunderstanding and mistrust, and foster a more profound sense of connection and compassion.

MOREOVER, reconciliation requires a willingness to engage in open and honest communication. This means being willing to listen with an open heart, expressing one's feelings and needs authentically, and engaging in dialogue grounded in respect, compassion, and mutual understanding. Effective communication is essential for clarifying misunderstandings, addressing grievances, and exploring pathways toward reconciliation.

IN ESSENCE, reconciliation is a profoundly transformative process beyond simply patching surface-level conflicts. It involves a profound shift in perspective, a willingness to let go of pride and ego, and a commitment to healing and growth. From a spiritual standpoint, reconciliation is about embodying the principles of love and compassion and recognizing the inherent worth and dignity of every individual involved. Through reconciliation, estranged parties can find healing, forgiveness, and a renewed sense of connection and wholeness.

GRACE

Grace, in its essence, transcends human understanding, embodying the boundless love and compassion of a Higher Power towards all beings. It serves as the bedrock upon which spiritual healing finds its footing, offering a profound sense of solace, acceptance, and renewal to those who seek it.

AT ITS CORE, grace represents the unmerited gift of love, compassion, and forgiveness bestowed upon individuals by a Higher Power. Unlike human notions of deserving or earning, grace operates outside meritocracy, extending its blessings freely and without condition. It reminds us that worthiness is inherent to everyone, regardless of past mistakes, shortcomings, or inadequacies.

FROM A SPIRITUAL PERSPECTIVE, grace is not merely a concept but a living, breathing force permeating all life aspects. It is the gentle whisper of hope in times of despair, the guiding light in moments of darkness, and the outstretched hand of compassion amidst the trials and tribulations of the human journey. Grace offers a pathway to redemption and renewal, inviting individuals to release guilt, shame, and self-condemnation and embrace the possibility of transformation and growth.

· · ·

MOREOVER, grace is a source of hope and inspiration, infusing life with meaning, purpose, and significance. It reminds us that no matter how lost or broken one may feel, divine love and compassion are ever-present, guiding individuals toward healing, wholeness, and spiritual fulfillment. In the face of adversity, grace offers a beacon of light, illuminating the path forward and instilling a sense of courage, resilience, and optimism.

IN RELATIONSHIPS, grace is pivotal in fostering reconciliation, forgiveness, and understanding. It encourages individuals to extend compassion and forgiveness to others, even in the face of hurt and betrayal, recognizing all beings' inherent dignity and humanity. By embodying the principles of grace, individuals can transcend the cycle of resentment and bitterness and forge pathways toward healing and reconciliation.

ULTIMATELY, grace is a testament to the boundless love and compassion of a Higher Power towards all creation. It is a reminder that no matter how far one may have strayed from their true path, divine love remains steadfast and unwavering, offering hope, redemption, and renewal to all who seek it. In embracing the transformative power of grace, individuals can find solace, acceptance, and healing and embark on a journey toward spiritual wholeness and fulfillment. From a spiritual perspective, grace is a divine force that permeates all aspects of life, offering hope, redemption, and renewal to those who seek it.

INTEGRATING spirituality into healing practices involves cultivating a daily spiritual routine that nourishes the soul and fosters inner growth. This may include prayer, meditation, scripture study, or acts of service and compassion. Through these practices, individuals deepen their connection to their spiritual beliefs and draw strength and guidance from a Higher Power.

PRAYER IS a cornerstone of spiritual healing. It is a sacred dialogue between individuals and their Creator, a means of expressing gratitude, seeking guidance, and finding solace in times of distress. Through prayer, individuals surrender their fears and worries to a Higher Power, trusting in divine wisdom and providence to guide them through difficult times.

MEDITATION IS another powerful tool for spiritual healing. It involves quieting the mind, focusing on the present moment, and cultivating inner peace and stillness. Through meditation, individuals cultivate mindfulness and self-awareness, gaining insight into their thoughts, emotions, and reactions. Meditation allows individuals to connect with their innermost selves and access a place of calm and clarity amidst the chaos of life.

SCRIPTURE STUDY IS a source of inspiration and guidance for many individuals on their spiritual healing journey. Sacred texts contain timeless wisdom, teachings, and stories that offer solace, encouragement, and hope. Through scripture study, individuals find comfort in the promises of faith, draw strength from the examples of spiritual leaders and prophets, and discover practical guidance for navigating life's challenges.

ACTS OF SERVICE and compassion are integral to spiritual healing. They involve reaching out to others in kindness, empathy, and love, offering support, encouragement, and companionship to those in need. Through acts of service, individuals embody the principles of love and compassion taught by their spiritual traditions, fostering connection, belonging, and healing within their communities.

INTEGRATING spirituality into healing practices provides individuals with a profound framework for understanding and navigating the complexities of estrangement. Through principles of forgiveness, reconciliation, and grace, individuals embark on a transformative journey of inner growth and renewal. Individuals draw strength, guidance, and hope from a Higher Power as they walk the path of healing and reconciliation by cultivating a daily spiritual routine that nourishes the soul and fosters inner connection.

THE EXPERIENCE of estrangement unfolds as a profound odyssey of self-discovery and growth, beckoning individuals to delve deeper into the reservoirs of their innermost being. Embracing spiritual resources opens a gateway to profound insights and revelations, guiding them through the labyrinthine passages of emotional turmoil and existential questioning. As they navigate this intricate terrain, connecting with the sacred essence within and without, they unearth reservoirs of resilience, fortitude, and compassion that empower them to transcend adversity and embrace their circumstances with renewed vigor and purpose.

ENGAGING with faith-based communities enriches this experience, offering a tapestry of support, wisdom, and shared experiences that serve as beacons of light in times of darkness. Within the sanctuaries of congregations and spiritual gatherings, individuals find kindred spirits who walk alongside them, offering empathy, understanding, and solidarity in the face of familial discord. Through communal prayers, rituals, and fellowship, they forge bonds of kinship and solidarity, weaving a safety net of love and acceptance that cushions their path and uplifts their spirits.

. . .

WITH EACH PRAYER WHISPERED, each meditation practiced, and each act of compassion extended, they anchor themselves firmly in the divine embrace, finding solace in the knowledge that they are held and cherished by a force greater than themselves.

IN ESSENCE, estrangement is not merely a passage of separation and loss but a profound quest for meaning, connection, and transcendence. Through the cultivation of spiritual resources, the nurturing embrace of faith-based communities, and the integration of spirituality into their healing endeavors, individuals embark on a transformative odyssey of self-discovery, healing, and reconciliation, guided by the timeless wisdom of the divine and the boundless power of the human spirit.

Types of Therapy and Benefits of Therapy

SEEKING professional therapy can be an invaluable step for individuals navigating the challenges of estrangement. Therapy offers a safe and supportive space to explore emotions, process experiences, and develop coping strategies. Several types of treatment can be particularly beneficial for individuals dealing with estrangement:

. . .

1. Cognitive Behavioral Therapy (CBT)

Cognitive Behavioral Therapy (CBT) is a widely used therapeutic approach that identifies and changes negative thought patterns and behaviors. CBT helps individuals develop healthier coping mechanisms and resilience by addressing maladaptive thinking.

BENEFITS OF **CBT**:

- It helps individuals identify and challenge negative thought patterns.
- Teaches practical coping strategies for managing stress and anxiety.
- Promotes emotional regulation and resilience.
- Encourages the development of healthier relationships and communication skills.

EXAMPLE: A person experiencing estrangement from a family member may struggle with negative thoughts such as "I am unlovable" or "This is all my fault." Through CBT, they can learn to recognize and challenge these thoughts, replacing them with more balanced and constructive beliefs, such as "I am worthy of love and respect" and "There are many factors that contributed to this situation."

. . .

2. Psychodynamic Therapy

Psychodynamic therapy delves into the unconscious mind to uncover unresolved conflicts and past experiences that influence present behavior and emotions. This approach helps individuals gain insight into their relational patterns and emotional responses.

BENEFITS OF PSYCHODYNAMIC THERAPY:

- Provides deep insight into unconscious processes and unresolved conflicts.
- It helps individuals understand the root causes of their emotional struggles.
- Fosters self-awareness and personal growth.
- Encourages the exploration of past experiences and their impact on current relationships.

EXAMPLE: A person estranged from their parents may discover through psychodynamic therapy that their feelings of abandonment and rejection stem from early childhood experiences of neglect. By gaining insight into these unconscious patterns, they can begin to heal and develop healthier relationships in the present.

3. Family Therapy

Family therapy involves working with multiple family members to improve communication, resolve conflicts, and strengthen relationships. This approach can be particularly beneficial for estranged families seeking to rebuild trust and connection.

BENEFITS OF FAMILY THERAPY:

- Improves communication and understanding among family members.
- Addresses and resolves conflicts and misunderstandings.
- Fosters a sense of unity and cooperation.
- Encourages the development of healthy boundaries and relational patterns.

EXAMPLE: A family experiencing estrangement between siblings may participate in family therapy to address underlying issues such as perceived favoritism, competition, and unresolved conflicts. The family can learn to communicate more effectively through guided discussions and exercises, express their needs and feelings, and work toward reconciliation.

4. Narrative Therapy

Narrative therapy focuses on helping individuals reframe their life stories and develop a more empowering narrative. This approach emphasizes the importance of personal meaning and the power of storytelling in shaping one's identity and experiences.

Benefits of Narrative Therapy:

- Empower individuals to reshape their narratives.
- Encourages the exploration of alternative perspectives and meanings.
- It fosters a sense of agency and control over one's life story.
- Promotes resilience and a positive self-concept.

Example: An individual who feels defined by their estrangement from a parent may work with a narrative therapist to explore alternative narratives, such as focusing on their resilience, strengths, and personal growth. By reframing their story, they can develop a more empowering and hopeful outlook.

5. Solution-Focused Brief Therapy (SFBT)

Solution-Focused Brief Therapy (SFBT) is a goal-oriented approach that emphasizes finding practical solutions to specific problems. This therapy focuses on identifying strengths and resources and developing actionable steps toward positive change.

BENEFITS OF **SFBT**:

- Promotes a positive and solution-oriented mindset.
- Encourages the identification and utilization of strengths and resources.
- Provides practical tools for addressing specific challenges.
- Focuses on achieving short-term goals and tangible results.

EXAMPLE: A person struggling with hopelessness due to estrangement may work with an SFBT therapist to identify small, achievable goals that can help improve their well-being, such as reconnecting with supportive friends, engaging in self-care activities, or exploring new hobbies and interests.

6. Mindfulness-Based Therapy

Mindfulness-based therapy incorporates mindfulness practices such as meditation, deep breathing, and body awareness to help individuals cultivate present-moment awareness and emotional regulation. This approach can reduce stress and promote a sense of calm and balance.

BENEFITS OF MINDFULNESS-BASED THERAPY:

- Enhances emotional regulation and stress management.
- Promotes present-moment awareness and mindfulness.
- Reduces symptoms of anxiety and depression.
- Encourages self-compassion and self-acceptance.

EXAMPLE: An individual experiencing anxiety and rumination due to estrangement may benefit from mindfulness-based therapy, learning techniques such as mindfulness meditation and mindful breathing to calm their mind, reduce stress, and cultivate a sense of inner peace.

Finding and Accessing Therapy

FINDING and accessing therapy can be crucial to healing and recovery for individuals navigating estrangement. Here are some practical steps and resources for finding and engaging in treatment:

1. Identifying Your Needs and Preferences

Before seeking therapy, it's essential to identify your specific needs and preferences. Consider the following questions:

- What are your primary concerns and goals for treatment?
- Do you prefer a particular type of therapy (e.g., CBT, psychodynamic, family therapy)?
- Are you looking for individual therapy, couples therapy, or family therapy?
- Do you have any preferences regarding the therapist's gender, cultural background, or therapeutic approach?

2. Researching Therapists and Therapy Options

Researching therapists and therapy options is essential for finding a good fit. Here are some ways to start your search:

- **Online Directories**: Websites such as Psychology Today, TherapyDen, and GoodTherapy offer searchable directories of licensed therapists, allowing you to filter by location, specialty, and therapy type.

- **Referrals**: Ask for referrals from trusted friends, family members, or healthcare providers who may recommend reputable therapists.
- **Insurance Providers**: Check with your insurance provider for a list of in-network therapists and coverage options for mental health services.
- **Community Resources**: Local mental health clinics, community centers, and religious organizations often offer therapy services or can provide referrals to therapists in your area.

3. Initial Consultations

Many therapists offer initial consultations, either for free or at a reduced cost. These consultations allow you to assess whether the therapist is a good fit for your needs and preferences. During the consultation, consider asking the following questions:

- What is their therapeutic approach and experience with estrangement issues?
- What is their availability and scheduling flexibility?
- What are their fees, and do they accept insurance or offer sliding-scale payment options?

- How comfortable do you feel discussing your concerns with the therapist?

4. Online and Teletherapy Options

With the rise of digital technology, online and teletherapy options have become increasingly accessible. These virtual therapy sessions can be conducted via video, phone, or secure messaging platforms, offering convenience and flexibility. Some popular online therapy platforms include:

- BetterHelp
- Talkspace
- Amwell
- 7 Cups

5. Community and Low-Cost Therapy Resources

Community and low-cost therapy resources can be valuable for individuals with financial constraints. Consider exploring the following options:

- **Sliding Scale Clinics**: Many community mental health clinics offer sliding scale fees based on income, making therapy more affordable.
- **University Counseling Centers**: Universities often have counseling centers that provide low-

cost or free therapy services to students and sometimes to the community.

- **Nonprofit Organizations**: Some nonprofit organizations offer free or low-cost therapy services to specific populations, such as survivors of domestic violence, LGBTQ+ individuals, or military veterans.

6. Employee Assistance Programs (EAPs)

Many employers offer Employee Assistance Programs (EAPs) that provide confidential counseling services to employees and their families. EAPs typically offer limited free therapy sessions and can refer to long-term therapy options. Check with your HR department to see if your employer offers an EAP.

7. Self-Help and Support Resources

In addition to therapy, self-help and support resources can provide valuable guidance and support for individuals navigating estrangement. Consider exploring the following:

- **Books and Workbooks**: Numerous self-help books and workbooks offer practical strategies for coping with estrangement, building resilience, and fostering healing.

- **Support Groups**: Online and in-person support groups provide a space for individuals to connect with others facing similar challenges, share experiences, and offer mutual support.
- **Educational Workshops and Webinars**: Many mental health organizations and therapists offer workshops and webinars on estrangement, communication, and emotional well-being.

The Benefits of Therapy for Estrangement

THERAPY OFFERS many benefits for individuals dealing with estrangement, providing a supportive and nonjudgmental space to explore emotions, develop coping strategies, and work toward healing and reconciliation. Some of the key benefits of therapy for estrangement include:

1. Emotional Support and Validation

Therapists provide a safe and compassionate space where individuals can express their feelings and experiences without fear of judgment. This emotional support and validation can be immensely comforting, helping individuals feel heard, understood, and accepted.

2. Insight and Self-Awareness

Therapy fosters greater insight and self-awareness by helping individuals explore their emotions, thoughts, and behaviors. This self-exploration can reveal underlying patterns, beliefs, and triggers contributing to estrangement, allowing individuals to understand themselves better and their relationships.

3. Coping Strategies and Tools

Therapists equip individuals with practical coping strategies and tools for managing stress, anxiety, and other emotional challenges. These techniques can include mindfulness practices, cognitive-behavioral exercises, and relaxation techniques that promote emotional regulation and resilience.

4. Improved Communication and Conflict Resolution

Effective communication and conflict resolution are essential for healing estranged relationships. Therapists teach individuals active listening, assertive communication, and nonviolent conflict resolution skills, helping them constructively navigate challenging conversations and address misunderstandings.

5. Healing and Reconciliation

Therapy can guide individuals through healing and reconciliation, whether with estranged family members or within themselves. Therapy fosters emotional healing and the possibility of renewed connections by addressing unresolved conflicts, processing past traumas, and exploring pathways toward forgiveness and understanding.

6. Personal Growth and Empowerment

Therapy is a transformative journey of personal growth and empowerment. Through it, individuals develop a deeper understanding of themselves, build resilience, and cultivate a sense of agency and control over their lives. This empowerment enables them to navigate estrangement's challenges more confidently and gracefully.

7. Building Healthy Boundaries

Setting and maintaining healthy boundaries is crucial for emotional well-being and self-respect. Therapists help individuals identify their needs and limits, develop assertiveness skills, and establish boundaries that protect their mental and emotional health.

EXAMPLES OF FINDING AND DOING THERAPY

Example 1: Finding a Therapist Through Online Directories

Sarah has been struggling with feelings of guilt and sadness due to her estrangement from her adult daughter.

She decides to seek professional therapy to help her cope with these emotions. Sarah starts by searching for therapists in her area using an online directory like Psychology Today. She filters the search results by location, specialty (estrangement), and therapy type (CBT). After reviewing several profiles, she finds a therapist who seems like a good fit and offers an initial consultation. Sarah feels comfortable with the therapist's approach during the consultation and decides to schedule regular sessions.

EXAMPLE 2: Accessing Therapy Through an EAP

John works for a large corporation that offers an Employee Assistance Program (EAP). He has been experiencing stress and anxiety due to estrangement from his siblings and wants to seek professional help. John contacts the EAP and is connected with a counselor who provides short-term therapy sessions. After a few sessions, John and the counselor determined that he would benefit from longer-term therapy. The EAP counselor refers John to a local therapist specializing in family estrangement, and John continues his therapy journey with their support.

EXAMPLE 3: Participating in Family Therapy

Lisa and her two adult sons have been estranged for several years due to unresolved conflicts and communication breakdowns. They decide to participate in family therapy to work towards reconciliation. Lisa contacts a family therapist with experience in estranged families and schedules an initial session. During the therapy sessions, the therapist facilitates open and honest communication, helping Lisa and her sons express their feelings and address their conflicts. Through family therapy, they gradually rebuild trust and strengthen their relationships.

Example 4: Engaging in Online Therapy

Michael lives in a rural area with limited access to in-person therapy services. He has been struggling with feelings of anger and resentment due to his estrangement from his parents. Michael decides to try online therapy and signs up for a platform like BetterHelp. He is matched with a licensed therapist who specializes in anger management and family issues. Through video sessions, Michael and his therapist work on identifying the root causes of his anger, developing coping strategies, and exploring pathways toward forgiveness and healing.

Example 5: Joining a Support Group

Due to her estrangement from her siblings, Emily has been feeling isolated and alone. She decides to join a support group for individuals dealing with family estrangement. Emily finds a local support group through a community mental health center and attends weekly meetings. In the support group, Emily connects with others who share similar experiences, receives emotional support, and learns new coping strategies. The sense of community and understanding helps Emily feel less alone and more empowered to navigate her estrangement journey.

EXAMPLE 6: Utilizing Sliding Scale Clinics

James is a college student with limited financial resources and has been experiencing depression due to estrangement from his father. He learns about a sliding scale clinic at his university counseling center that offers affordable therapy services. James schedules an appointment with a counselor and begins weekly therapy sessions. The counselor helps James explore the underlying causes of his depression, develop healthy coping mechanisms, and work toward healing and reconciliation with his father.

THERAPY OFFERS many benefits for individuals navigating the challenges of estrangement. Whether through individual therapy, family therapy, or support groups, therapy provides a safe and supportive space to explore emotions, develop coping strategies, and work toward healing and reconciliation. By seeking therapy and utilizing available resources, individuals can empower themselves to navigate the complexities of estrangement with greater resilience, understanding, and hope.

CHAPTER 5
EXPERT INSIGHTS AND PERSPECTIVES

~

E strangement, a multifaceted and intricate occurrence, has captured the interest of experts from diverse disciplines, each contributing valuable insights and perspectives to illuminate its complex dynamics and far-reaching implications. In this chapter, we embark on a comprehensive exploration of the psychological, legal, and cultural dimensions of estrangement. By delving into these multifaceted aspects, we endeavor to deepen our understanding of this phenomenon, uncovering the nuanced factors that contribute to it, examining effective strategies for coping and fostering healing, addressing pertinent legal considerations, and contextualizing estranged relationships within the broader societal and cultural landscape.

Psychological Perspectives: Understanding the Dynamics of Estrangement

Attachment Theory and Estrangement

Psychology and neuroscience offer profound insights into the intricate dynamics of estranged relationships, delving into the interplay of emotions, behaviors, and cognitive processes. At the core of psychological inquiry lies attachment theory, which posits that early experiences with caregivers shape individuals' attachment styles, influencing their interpersonal dynamics throughout life. Insecure attachment styles characterized by ambivalence, avoidance, or anxiety can hinder the formation of secure connections, contributing to difficulties in maintaining relationships and, ultimately, estrangement.

Attachment theory, initially developed by John Bowlby and later expanded by Mary Ainsworth, emphasizes the importance of early bonding experiences in shaping individuals' emotional and relational frameworks. Secure attachment, formed through consistent and responsive caregiving, fosters a sense of safety and trust in relationships. In contrast, insecure attachment styles—anxious, avoidant, and disorganized —emerge from inconsistent or unresponsive caregiving, leading to challenges in forming and maintaining healthy relationships.

. . .

A HEIGHTENED NEED for reassurance and fear of abandonment characterizes anxious attachment. Individuals with an anxious attachment may become overly dependent on their relationships, seeking constant validation and fearing rejection. This attachment style can contribute to estrangement when their intense emotional needs overwhelm their relationships, leading to conflicts and eventual distancing.

ON THE OTHER HAND, avoidant attachment involves a tendency to distance oneself emotionally from others. Individuals with avoidant attachment may have learned to suppress their emotional needs due to early experiences of neglect or rejection. This detachment can result in difficulties forming deep connections, leading to estrangement as they withdraw from relationships to protect themselves from potential emotional pain.

DISORGANIZED ATTACHMENT IS a combination of anxious and avoidant behaviors, often resulting from traumatic or inconsistent caregiving. Individuals with disorganized attachment may exhibit contradictory behaviors, seeking closeness while simultaneously pushing others away. This ambivalence can create chaotic and unstable relationships, increasing the likelihood of estrangement.

. . .

Understanding these attachment styles provides valuable insights into the emotional and relational patterns contributing to estrangement. By identifying and addressing these underlying attachment dynamics, psychologists can help individuals develop healthier relationship patterns and navigate the complexities of estranged relationships.

Benefits:

- **Self-Awareness**: Understanding one's attachment style can lead to greater self-awareness and identifying patterns contributing to estrangement.
- **Healing Relationships**: Knowledge of attachment theory can facilitate the development of healthier relationships by addressing underlying insecurities.

Example:

- **John and His Mother**: John's avoidant attachment style, stemming from a childhood of emotional neglect, led to a strained relationship with his mother. Through therapy focused on attachment theory, John learned to recognize his tendency to withdraw emotionally and began to rebuild a more open and supportive relationship with his mother.

Communication Breakdown and Emotional Needs

EFFECTIVE COMMUNICATION IS foundational to healthy relationships. When communication breaks down, misunderstandings and misinterpretations can arise, leading to unresolved conflicts and emotional distance. Common communication barriers include defensiveness, stonewalling, criticism, and contempt. These patterns create a toxic cycle in which unresolved conflicts and unmet emotional needs accumulate, contributing to estrangement.

BENEFITS:

- **Conflict Resolution**: Learning effective communication techniques can help resolve conflicts and prevent estrangement.
- **Emotional Healing**: Improved communication can foster emotional healing and rebuild trust.

EXAMPLE:

- **Alice and Her Sister**: Alice and her sister were estranged due to constant misunderstandings and arguments. By participating in family therapy, learning to use "I" statements, and reflective listening, they addressed their unresolved issues and rebuilt their relationship.

The Emotional Toll of Estrangement

INDIVIDUALS GRAPPLING with estrangement experience a range of intense emotions, from grief and anger to guilt, shame, and loneliness. The rupture of once-close relationships can evoke profound loss and sadness, while unresolved conflicts and perceived betrayals fuel resentment and hatred.

BENEFITS:

- **Emotional Resilience**: Understanding the emotional impact of estrangement can help individuals develop resilience and coping strategies.
- **Mental Health Support**: Awareness of the emotional toll can encourage individuals to seek mental health support and improve their well-being.

. . .

EXAMPLE:

- **Emma's Journey**: Emma experienced profound grief and anger after becoming estranged from her father. Through therapy, she learned to process these emotions and gradually found peace and forgiveness, improving her overall mental health.

~

Coping Mechanisms and Healing Strategies

PSYCHOLOGISTS EXPLORE effective coping mechanisms and healing strategies to support individuals navigating estranged relationships. These strategies include Cognitive-Behavioral Therapy (CBT), mindfulness and self-compassion, family therapy, and support groups.

BENEFITS:

- **Practical Tools**: Individuals gain practical tools and techniques to manage emotions and improve relationships.
- **Support Systems**: Access to support systems and therapy can provide guidance and encouragement for healing.

. . .

EXAMPLE:

- **Mike's Support Network**: Mike, estranged from his close friend, joined a support group where he found understanding and validation. He also engaged in mindfulness practices that helped him manage his stress and emotional pain, leading to a healthier mindset.

~

Cognitive-behavioral therapy (CBT)

CBT HELPS individuals identify and challenge negative thought patterns and beliefs contributing to their emotional distress. By reframing these thoughts and developing healthier coping mechanisms, individuals can reduce feelings of anxiety, depression, and anger associated with estrangement.

BENEFITS:

- **Improved Mental Health**: CBT can help individuals manage symptoms of anxiety and depression.

- **Positive Coping Strategies**: CBT provides practical tools for reframing negative thoughts and developing healthier coping mechanisms.

EXAMPLE:

- **Jane's Transformation**: After estranging herself from her mother, Jane struggled with feelings of inadequacy and self-blame. Through CBT, she learned to challenge these negative beliefs and develop a more positive self-image, leading to improved mental health and self-confidence.

Mindfulness and Self-Compassion

MINDFULNESS PRACTICES like meditation and deep breathing can help individuals stay present and manage their emotions. Self-compassion involves treating oneself with kindness and understanding, reducing feelings of guilt and shame, and promoting emotional healing.

BENEFITS:

- **Emotional Regulation**: Mindfulness practices help individuals manage their emotions and reduce stress.
- **Self-Compassion**: Developing self-compassion can reduce guilt and shame and promote emotional healing.

EXAMPLE:

- **Tom's Journey**: After estranging himself from his father, Tom felt overwhelmed by guilt and shame. By practicing mindfulness and self-compassion, he learned to treat himself with kindness and understanding, reducing guilt and improving his emotional well-being.

Family Therapy

FAMILY THERAPY PROVIDES a structured environment for estranged family members to address their conflicts and work toward reconciliation. A trained therapist facilitates open and constructive dialogue, helping family members understand each other's perspectives and develop healthier communication patterns.

· · ·

BENEFITS:

- **Conflict Resolution**: Family therapy provides a safe space for addressing conflicts and misunderstandings.
- **Improved Relationships**: Family therapy can help rebuild trust and improve family communication.

EXAMPLE:

- **The Smith Family**: The family was estranged due to unresolved conflicts and communication breakdowns. Family therapy taught them to communicate effectively and address their issues, improving relationships and family harmony.

Support Groups

SUPPORT GROUPS OFFER a safe space for individuals to share their experiences and receive validation and support from others who understand their struggles. These groups can provide a sense of community and belonging, reducing feelings of isolation and loneliness.

. . .

BENEFITS:

- **Community Support**: Support groups provide a sense of community and belonging.
- **Emotional Validation**: Sharing experiences in a support group can provide validation and reduce feelings of isolation.

EXAMPLE:

- **Laura's Support Group**: Laura joined a support group for individuals experiencing estrangement and found a supportive community where she could share her story and receive encouragement. This support helped her feel less isolated and more hopeful about her future.

Legal Considerations: Navigating the Legal Landscape

INHERITANCE AND ESTRANGEMENT

Inheritance laws vary widely across jurisdictions, and estrangement can complicate matters related to the distribution of assets and property. Legal experts examine how estrangement impacts inheritance rights, exploring scenarios such as disinheritance, contested wills, and the rights of estranged heirs.

IN MANY LEGAL SYSTEMS, individuals can distribute their assets as they see fit through a will or estate plan. However, estrangement can lead to disputes and legal challenges if an individual decides to disinherit an estranged family member. Contested wills can result in lengthy legal battles, with estranged heirs seeking to challenge the will's validity or the distribution's fairness.

MOREOVER, legal experts explore the concept of "forced heirship" in certain jurisdictions, where laws mandate that a portion of an individual's estate must be left to specific family members, regardless of estrangement. Understanding these legal frameworks is essential for individuals navigating inheritance disputes and seeking to protect their rights and interests.

BENEFITS:

- **Legal Clarity**: Understanding inheritance laws can help individuals navigate disputes and protect their rights.

- **Preparedness**: Awareness of legal implications can encourage individuals to make informed decisions about their estate planning.

EXAMPLE:

- **The Johnson Family**: The Johnson family faced a legal battle over inheritance after the patriarch disinherited his estranged daughter. Legal mediation helped them reach a fair settlement, ensuring the daughter received her rightful share.

Custody and Parental Rights

ESTRANGEMENT CAN ALSO HAVE significant implications for custody and parental rights, particularly in cases of divorce or separation. Legal experts analyze how estrangement affects custody arrangements, visitation rights, and parental responsibilities, highlighting the complexities of navigating these legal issues.

IN CUSTODY DISPUTES, courts prioritize the child's best interests, considering factors such as the child's emotional and physical well-being, the relationship between the child and each parent, and the ability of each parent to provide a stable and nurturing environment. Estrangement can complicate these assessments, as courts must balance the child's need for a relationship with both parents against any potential harm caused by the estranged parent's behavior.

LEGAL EXPERTS also examine the impact of estrangement on parental responsibilities, such as child support and decision-making authority. Estranged parents may face challenges in fulfilling their legal obligations or maintaining meaningful involvement in their child's life, leading to further legal and emotional complexities.

BENEFITS:

- **Child's Best Interests**: Understanding custody laws ensures decisions are made in the child's best interests.
- **Parental Rights and Responsibilities**: Legal clarity helps estranged parents understand their rights and responsibilities.

EXAMPLE:

- **The Smith Divorce**: During the Smiths' high-conflict divorce, estrangement between the father and children complicated custody arrangements. Legal mediation helped create a balanced custody plan that prioritized the children's well-being while maintaining both parents' involvement.

Legal Interventions and Mediation

LEGAL INTERVENTIONS, such as mediation and family law proceedings, facilitate resolutions and mitigate conflicts within estranged families. Mediation offers a structured process for estranged parties to negotiate and reach mutually agreeable solutions with the assistance of a neutral mediator, potentially paving the way for reconciliation or amicable separation.

MEDIATION PROVIDES A LESS adversarial alternative to traditional litigation, allowing parties to address their conflicts in a confidential and supportive environment. The mediator facilitates open communication, helping parties identify their underlying needs and interests and explore potential solutions. By fostering constructive dialogue and collaboration, mediation can help estranged family members find common ground and work toward a resolution.

· · ·

IN ADDITION TO MEDIATION, legal experts explore other forms of alternative dispute resolution, such as collaborative law and arbitration, which offer additional options for resolving estranged family conflicts outside of court. These approaches emphasize cooperation and problem-solving, reducing litigation's emotional and financial costs and promoting healthier outcomes for all parties involved.

BENEFITS:

- **Conflict Resolution**: Mediation provides a structured process for resolving conflicts amicably.
- **Cost-Effective**: Alternative dispute resolution methods can reduce litigation's financial and emotional costs.

EXAMPLE:

- **Mediation Success**: In a high-conflict family dispute, mediation helped the parties reach a mutually acceptable agreement without resorting to lengthy and costly litigation. This resolution allowed them to move forward with their lives more peacefully.

Legal Advocacy and Support

UNDERSTANDING the legal dimensions of estrangement is essential for individuals navigating familial conflicts and legal professionals advocating on their behalf. By clarifying rights, responsibilities, and available legal remedies, legal experts empower individuals to make informed decisions and seek appropriate legal recourse in addressing the complexities of estranged relationships.

LEGAL ADVOCACY and support organizations are crucial in providing resources and assistance to individuals navigating estranged relationships. These organizations offer legal advice, representation, and support services, helping individuals understand their rights and navigate the legal system effectively.

FURTHERMORE, legal experts advocate for policy changes and reforms to address the unique challenges individuals experiencing estrangement face. By raising awareness and promoting legislative initiatives, legal professionals can contribute to developing more equitable and supportive legal frameworks for estranged families.

. . .

BENEFITS:

- **Legal Empowerment**: Understanding legal rights empowers individuals to navigate conflicts more effectively.
- **Support Resources**: Advocacy organizations provide essential resources and support.

EXAMPLE:

- **Legal Aid Success**: A legal aid organization helped Maria navigate a complex custody dispute, providing her with legal representation and support. This assistance enabled Maria to secure a fair custody arrangement and protect her child's best interests.

Cultural and Societal Factors: Navigating Stigma, Judgment, and Support Systems

THE IMPACT of Cultural Narratives

Across cultures, families are often regarded as fundamental units of social cohesion, emphasizing maintaining harmonious relationships and familial bonds. Estrangement challenges these ideals, disrupting societal expectations of unconditional familial support and raising questions about the boundaries of individual autonomy within familial contexts.

CULTURAL NARRATIVES SURROUNDING family and relationships play a significant role in shaping individuals' experiences of estrangement. Family loyalty, filial piety, and collective identity are highly valued in many cultures, leading to intense societal pressure to maintain familial ties despite conflicts or dysfunction. These cultural narratives can create a sense of obligation and guilt for individuals considering or experiencing estrangement, making it difficult for them to prioritize their well-being.

MOREOVER, cultural narratives often emphasize the importance of forgiveness and reconciliation, reinforcing that individuals should resolve conflicts and restore relationships at all costs. While these values can promote healing and connection, they can also place undue pressure on individuals to maintain relationships that may be harmful or abusive. Understanding these cultural dynamics is essential for developing culturally sensitive interventions and support systems that respect individuals' autonomy and well-being.

. . .

BENEFITS:

- **Cultural Sensitivity**: Understanding cultural narratives helps develop culturally sensitive interventions.
- **Reduced Pressure**: Awareness of cultural pressures can help individuals prioritize their well-being.

EXAMPLE:

- **Cultural Sensitivity in Therapy**: A therapist working with an individual from a culture emphasizing family loyalty helped clients navigate their feelings of obligation and guilt, fostering a more balanced approach to their familial relationships.

Societal Norms and Expectations

SOCIETAL NORMS and expectations regarding familial relationships significantly influence attitudes toward estrangement. Gender norms, for example, may dictate different expectations for men and women within familial relationships, shaping how estrangement is perceived and responded to based on gendered expectations of familial loyalty and responsibilities.

IN MANY CULTURES, women are often expected to prioritize family relationships and caregiving roles, leading to more significant societal pressure to maintain familial ties and resolve conflicts. Conversely, men may face different societal expectations regarding emotional expression and conflict resolution, influencing their experiences of estrangement.

RELIGIOUS BELIEFS and cultural traditions also play a significant role in shaping attitudes toward estrangement. Many spiritual and artistic traditions emphasize the sanctity of family ties and the importance of forgiveness and reconciliation, potentially exerting pressure on individuals to maintain familial relationships despite conflict or abuse. These cultural and religious values can create complex dynamics for individuals navigating estrangement, influencing their decisions and experiences.

BENEFITS:

- **Gender Sensitivity**: Understanding gender norms helps address gender-specific challenges in estranged relationships.

- **Cultural Awareness**: Awareness of religious and cultural influences helps develop supportive interventions.

EXAMPLE:

- **Gender-Sensitive Support**: A support group for women navigating estrangement provided gender-sensitive resources and support, helping members address societal pressures and prioritize their emotional well-being.

The Role of Support Systems and Resources

CULTURAL and societal factors also influence the availability and accessibility of support systems and resources for individuals navigating estrangement. In some cultures, tight-knit family structures and communal expectations may exacerbate feelings of guilt or obligation in estranged individuals. In contrast, in others, there may be greater acceptance of individual autonomy and boundary-setting within familial relationships.

· · ·

Support systems and resources for individuals experiencing estrangement vary widely across cultural contexts. These may include religious or spiritual communities, mental health services, support groups, online forums, or advocacy organizations. Sociologists study how cultural and societal norms influence individuals' access to these resources and how these resources are perceived and utilized within different cultural contexts.

Religious and spiritual communities can offer valuable support to individuals navigating estrangement, providing a sense of community and belonging, as well as guidance and counseling from religious leaders. However, these communities may also reinforce cultural and religious norms that emphasize familial loyalty and reconciliation, creating additional challenges for individuals seeking to establish healthy boundaries.

Mental health services, including therapy and counseling, support individuals experiencing estrangement. Access to mental health services can vary significantly depending on cultural and societal factors, with some communities offering robust support networks while others lack adequate resources. The stigma surrounding mental health issues and seeking professional help can also influence individuals' willingness to access these services.

. . .

Support groups and online forums offer safe spaces for individuals to share their experiences and receive validation and support from others who understand their struggles. These groups can provide valuable resources and coping strategies, reducing feelings of isolation and promoting emotional healing.

Advocacy organizations are crucial in raising awareness and providing resources and support to individuals navigating estrangement. These organizations offer legal advice, representation, and support services, helping individuals understand their rights and effectively navigate the complexities of estranged relationships.

Benefits:

- **Community Support**: Access to support systems and resources fosters a sense of community and belonging.
- **Emotional Healing**: Support systems provide validation and coping strategies, promoting emotional healing.

Example:

- **Online Support Forum**: An online forum for individuals experiencing estrangement provided a safe space for sharing experiences and receiving support. Members found validation and practical advice, helping them navigate their challenges more effectively.

Navigating Stigma and Judgment

ESTRANGEMENT, the deliberate distancing or cutting off of ties between family members or significant others, is a phenomenon laden with social stigma and often accompanied by judgment, criticism, and even social ostracism. In many societies, family unity and filial piety hold immense cultural significance, making estrangement from family members particularly challenging and fraught with emotional turmoil.

ONE OF THE primary reasons for the stigma surrounding estrangement lies in societal norms and expectations regarding family relationships. Across cultures, families are often regarded as the bedrock of social cohesion, emphasizing maintaining harmonious relationships and familial bonds. Estrangement disrupts this idealized notion of familial unity, challenging deeply ingrained beliefs about the unconditional love and support that family members are expected to provide. Consequently, individuals who choose to estrange themselves from family members may be viewed with skepticism, seen as deviating from societal norms, and even criticized for their decisions.

FURTHERMORE, cultural factors such as gender norms, religious beliefs, and cultural traditions can significantly influence attitudes toward estrangement. Gender roles, for instance, may dictate different expectations for men and women within family dynamics, affecting how estrangement is perceived and responded to based on gender. Similarly, religious beliefs and cultural traditions often emphasize the sanctity of family ties and the importance of forgiveness and reconciliation, potentially exerting pressure on individuals to maintain familial relationships despite conflict or abuse.

MOREOVER, the decision to estrange oneself from family members can evoke shame, guilt, and social isolation, particularly in cultures where familial bonds are revered and prioritized above individual autonomy. Individuals may fear being judged by their peers, labeled as disrespectful or disloyal, and may even face exclusion or ostracism from family-centric communities. This social stigma surrounding estrangement can exacerbate the emotional distress already experienced by individuals grappling with the complexities of family conflict and dysfunction.

. . .

DESPITE THE CHALLENGES posed by social stigma, it is essential to recognize that estrangement is not inherently harmful or indicative of moral failure. In many cases, estrangement may be a necessary act of self-preservation, undertaken to protect one's emotional well-being and establish healthy boundaries in the face of toxic or abusive family dynamics. By challenging societal norms and promoting understanding and empathy towards individuals navigating estrangement, communities can create more inclusive and supportive environments where individuals feel empowered to make decisions that align with their needs and values.

BENEFITS:

- **Reduced Stigma**: Challenging societal norms can reduce the stigma associated with estrangement.
- **Empowerment**: Empowering individuals to prioritize their well-being and make decisions that align with their values.

EXAMPLE:

- **Community Awareness Campaign**: A community awareness campaign focused on challenging the stigma of estrangement helped foster a more supportive environment for individuals navigating familial conflicts. The campaign promoted understanding and empathy, reducing the social pressure to maintain harmful relationships.

∾

Fostering Empathy and Understanding

FOSTERING empathy and understanding towards individuals navigating estrangement involves challenging societal norms and promoting awareness and acceptance of diverse family dynamics. By creating inclusive and supportive environments, communities can empower individuals to prioritize their well-being and navigate familial conflicts with resilience and compassion.

EDUCATIONAL INITIATIVES and public awareness campaigns can challenge stigma and promote understanding of estrangement. These initiatives can foster more inclusive and supportive communities by raising awareness of the complexities of estranged relationships and highlighting the importance of individual autonomy and emotional well-being.

. . .

S<small>UPPORT GROUPS</small> and advocacy organizations also play a vital role in providing resources and support to individuals navigating estrangement. By offering safe spaces for individuals to share their experiences and receive validation and support, these groups can help reduce feelings of isolation and promote emotional healing.

B<small>ENEFITS</small>:

- **Increased Empathy**: Promoting empathy and understanding can create more inclusive and supportive communities.
- **Emotional Support**: Support groups provide safe spaces for sharing experiences and receiving validation.

E<small>XAMPLE</small>:

- **Empathy Workshop**: An empathy workshop for community leaders helped raise awareness of the challenges individuals face navigating estrangement. The workshop promoted understanding and encouraged the development of supportive community programs.

The Role of Media and Representation

MEDIA AND REPRESENTATION also play a significant role in shaping societal attitudes towards estrangement. Portrayals of estranged relationships in literature, film, and television can influence public perceptions and normalize diverse family dynamics.

POSITIVE AND NUANCED representations of estranged relationships can challenge stigma and promote empathy and understanding. Media representations can foster greater awareness and acceptance of diverse family dynamics by highlighting the complexities and emotional challenges faced by individuals experiencing estrangement.

BENEFITS:

- **Challenging Stigma**: Positive media representations can challenge stigma and promote empathy.
- **Increased Awareness**: Media portrayals can raise awareness of the complexities of estranged relationships.

EXAMPLE:

- **Television Drama**: A popular television drama featured a storyline about a character navigating estrangement from their family. The show's nuanced portrayal of the character's emotional journey helped raise awareness and promote empathy among viewers.

ESTRANGEMENT IS a multifaceted phenomenon influenced by psychological, legal, and cultural factors that shape individuals' experiences and perceptions within familial relationships. By integrating insights from psychology, sociology, and cultural studies, we gain a comprehensive understanding of the complexities of estrangement, highlighting the emotional dynamics, legal considerations, and cultural nuances that contribute to its pervasive impact.

THIS CHAPTER UNDERSCORES the importance of interdisciplinary perspectives in elucidating the intricate dynamics of estrangement and informing compassionate responses to support individuals and families navigating estranged relationships. By fostering awareness, empathy, and informed dialogue, we can cultivate inclusive and supportive communities where individuals feel empowered to prioritize their emotional well-being and navigate familial conflicts with resilience and compassion.

· · ·

THIS CHAPTER PROVIDES valuable guidance for individuals experiencing estrangement through expert insights and perspectives. It offers practical strategies for coping, fostering healing, and navigating the legal and cultural complexities of estranged relationships. By embracing a holistic approach that considers estrangement's psychological, legal, and cultural dimensions, we can better support individuals on their journey toward healing, reconciliation, and personal growth.

BENEFITS:

- **Comprehensive Understanding**: This chapter thoroughly explains estrangement's psychological, legal, and cultural dimensions.
- **Practical Strategies**: The chapter offers practical strategies for coping, fostering healing, and navigating the complexities of estranged relationships.
- **Support and Empathy**: By promoting awareness, empathy, and informed dialogue, the chapter fosters a supportive environment for individuals experiencing estrangement.

EXAMPLE:

- **Holistic Support**: An individual navigating estrangement used the insights and strategies from this chapter to seek therapy, join a support group, and engage in legal mediation. This holistic approach helped them manage their emotional distress, rebuild relationships, and navigate legal challenges, leading to a more balanced and fulfilling life.

By EXPANDING each segment of this chapter, we provide a comprehensive exploration of estrangement, highlighting its multifaceted nature and offering valuable insights and strategies for individuals navigating this complex phenomenon. This expanded chapter aims to empower individuals with knowledge, support, and practical tools to manage their experiences of estrangement and foster healing and reconciliation.

CHAPTER 6

ACCEPTANCE WHEN RECONCILIATION ISN'T POSSIBLE: ACCEPTANCE, CLOSURE, AND MOVING FORWARD

~

Embracing Acceptance: Acknowledging Reality and Letting Go

In the intricate and often turbulent landscape of estranged relationships, there inevitably arrives a juncture where reconciliation appears increasingly remote, if not entirely implausible. Embracing acceptance within this context constitutes a profoundly introspective and emotionally charged endeavor, necessitating individuals to confront the stark reality that the hope for reconciliation may need to be relinquished. This process involves a profound acknowledgment of the limitations inherent within the relationship dynamic and a deliberate decision to release the grip of expectation and desire for reconciliation.

. . .

AT ITS CORE, embracing acceptance demands a courageous confrontation with the painful truth that certain relationships may remain irreparably fractured despite one's earnest efforts and sincere wishes. It requires individuals to grapple with the dissonance between their deeply cherished aspirations for reconciliation and the harsh realities of unresolved conflicts, irreconcilable differences, or entrenched patterns of dysfunction within the relationship. This acknowledgment represents a significant departure from the idealized vision of harmony and unity that individuals may have harbored for their estranged relationships, compelling them to reconcile with human connection's inherent imperfections and limitations.

THE JOURNEY of embracing acceptance is fraught with emotional complexity, often giving rise to a kaleidoscope of feelings that can be overwhelming and disorienting. Central to this process is the recognition of loss — the loss of what once was, the loss of what could have been, and perhaps most poignantly, the loss of hope. This recognition engenders a profound sense of grief and mourning as individuals come to terms with the shattered dreams of reconciliation and the irretrievable moments of connection that now exist only in memory. The pain of this loss is often amplified by the realization that the envisioned future of reconciliation may forever remain elusive, leaving behind a void that can seem impossible.

ALONGSIDE GRIEF, acceptance may also evoke feelings of profound disappointment and disillusionment as individuals confront the stark contrast between their idealized expectations and the harsh realities of their estranged relationships. Disappointment arises from the recognition that despite their best intentions and earnest efforts, the desired outcome of reconciliation may remain beyond reach. This disappointment may be compounded by feelings of betrayal or abandonment, particularly if individuals had invested significant emotional energy and hope in the prospect of healing and renewal.

FURTHERMORE, embracing acceptance may entail confronting a complex array of emotions such as anger, resentment, and bitterness towards oneself, the estranged party, or external circumstances perceived to have contributed to the relationship breakdown. Anger may stem from a sense of injustice or betrayal as individuals grapple with feelings of hurt or abandonment inflicted by the actions or behaviors of the estranged party. Resentment may arise from the perceived unfairness of the situation or from the realization that one's efforts toward reconciliation have gone unrecognized or unreciprocated. Bitterness may linger as individuals struggle to reconcile their idealized visions of the relationship with the harsh realities of its demise, leading to disillusionment and cynicism towards the concept of reconciliation itself.

HOWEVER, amidst the tumult of these turbulent emotions, there may also be moments of profound relief — relief from the burden of uncertainty, the ceaseless cycle of hope and disappointment, and the emotional anguish of holding onto an elusive dream. Though tinged with sadness and resignation, this relief represents a pivotal turning point in the journey toward acceptance. It signifies the gradual relinquishment of the emotional attachments and expectations that have tethered individuals to the hope for reconciliation, paving the way for a more grounded and realistic appraisal of the relationship dynamic.

IN ADDITION to the emotional complexities inherent in the process of embracing acceptance, individuals may also grapple with a myriad of cognitive and existential challenges as they come to terms with the limitations of their estranged relationships. This may entail a profound existential reckoning with questions of identity, purpose, and belonging as individuals confront the unsettling realization that the narratives they once constructed around their relationships may no longer hold. It may also involve a process of cognitive restructuring as individuals endeavor to reconcile their idealized visions of the relationship with the stark realities of its demise, integrating the painful truths of their experiences into a coherent and meaningful narrative.

MOREOVER, embracing acceptance necessitates a fundamental shift in perspective — reframing the narrative surrounding the estranged relationship. It involves relinquishing the desire to rewrite the past or to force a reconciliation that may never come to fruition. Instead, it invites individuals to embrace the present moment, find solace in the inherent value of their emotional well-being, and chart a course toward personal growth and healing. This reframing of the narrative empowers individuals to reclaim agency over their own lives, recognizing that while they may not be able to control the actions or choices of others, they can still determine their responses and attitudes toward their circumstances.

IN ESSENCE, embracing acceptance in the face of irreconcilable estrangement is a profoundly transformative process that unfolds over time, often marked by moments of profound insight, catharsis, and growth. It demands courage, resilience, and self-compassion as individuals navigate the complex terrain of their own emotions and experiences, gradually accepting the limitations of their estranged relationships while embracing the possibilities of the future. Through this process, individuals can find a sense of closure and resolution, enabling them to move forward with renewed purpose and resilience, even in the aftermath of profound loss.

BENEFITS:

- **Emotional Relief:** Letting go of the hope for reconciliation can provide emotional relief, freeing individuals from unmet expectations.
- **Increased Clarity:** Acceptance fosters a clear-eyed view of the relationship, allowing individuals to make more informed decisions about their future.
- **Personal Growth:** Acceptance allows individuals to focus on their growth and well-being rather than being consumed by the hope for reconciliation.
- **Empowerment:** Embracing acceptance empowers individuals to take control of their emotional journey and make decisions that prioritize their well-being.

EXAMPLE:

- **Jane's Story:** Jane spent years hoping for reconciliation with her estranged sibling. After attending a support group, she realized acceptance was the only path to peace. By letting go of her expectations, Jane found emotional relief and clarity, allowing her to focus on her well-being and personal growth. Through acceptance, Jane could reclaim her sense of self and move forward with renewed purpose and resilience.

Finding Closure: Honoring Unresolved Emotions and Relationships

THE CONCEPT of closure often yearned for in the aftermath of estrangement, holds a profound significance in the journey toward healing and reconciliation. Within the intricate landscape of estranged relationships, individuals grapple with the profound loss and upheaval of severed ties with loved ones. Closure offers a beacon of hope amidst the tumultuous sea of emotions and uncertainties that follow the fracturing of familial or relational bonds, providing a pathway toward resolution and inner peace amidst the wreckage of shattered dreams and unfulfilled expectations.

CLOSURE ENCOMPASSES ACKNOWLEDGING and honoring unresolved emotions and relationships, offering individuals a means of finding a sense of completion and finality in the face of separation. While closure may not erase the lingering pain and heartache of estrangement, it serves as a guiding light, providing a semblance of relief and release and equipping individuals with the tools they need to navigate the complexities of their emotional landscape and move forward with greater clarity and purpose.

THE QUEST for closure represents a fundamental aspect of the healing journey for many individuals. It offers a means of coming to terms with the irreconcilable realities of their relationships and finding peace amidst the wreckage of shattered dreams and unfulfilled expectations. Within the labyrinth of emotions accompanying estrangement, individuals may turn to strategies in their quest for closure, each offering a unique pathway toward healing and reconciliation with the past.

ONE SUCH STRATEGY involves the therapeutic act of writing letters. This cathartic endeavor allows individuals to articulate thoughts, emotions, and grievances left unspoken amidst estrangement. Whether these letters are addressed to estranged loved ones or remain unsent, committing one's innermost thoughts to paper is a powerful release form, allowing individuals to confront their pain, express their truths, and begin letting go.

ENGAGING in rituals can also play a pivotal role in the journey towards closure, offering individuals a tangible means of honoring the significance of the relationships that have been lost while acknowledging their finality. Rituals can take myriad forms, from creating a symbolic ceremony to commemorate the end of a relationship to engaging in acts of remembrance or memorialization that pay homage to the bonds that once existed. These rituals give individuals a sense of closure and completion, allowing them to bid farewell to the past and embrace future possibilities with renewed clarity and purpose.

MOREOVER, therapy represents a valuable resource for individuals seeking closure in the wake of estrangement, offering a safe and supportive space to explore emotions, gain insights, and work toward acceptance. Within the therapeutic setting, individuals are provided with the opportunity to confront the complexities of their grief, navigate the intricacies of forgiveness, and confront the myriad emotions that accompany the process of letting go. A skilled therapist can serve as a compassionate guide, offering guidance and support as individuals grapple with the challenges of closure and embark on the journey toward healing and reconciliation with the past.

THROUGH THERAPY, individuals can begin to address unresolved issues, confront deep-seated emotions, and reframe their narratives surrounding the estranged relationships, ultimately finding a sense of closure and peace within themselves. By embracing acceptance and letting go of the hope for reconciliation, individuals can free themselves from the burdens of the past and embark on a journey toward self-discovery and renewal. In doing so, they can reclaim agency over their lives, honor the significance of their experiences, and move forward with a newfound sense of clarity, purpose, and resilience.

In essence, closure embodies the profound act of acknowledging and honoring the complexities of one's emotions and experiences in the aftermath of estrangement. It is a process that transcends mere acceptance of the irreparable nature of fractured relationships, encompassing a deeper understanding of the inherent humanity and imperfection that defines human connection. In embracing closure, individuals confront the harsh realities of estrangement with courage and resilience, allowing themselves to release the burdens of guilt, shame, and regret that often accompany severed ties with loved ones.

BENEFITS:

- **Emotional Resolution:** Finding closure helps individuals process and resolve lingering emotions, leading to emotional healing.
- **Personal Empowerment:** Closure empowers individuals to take control of their emotional journey, fostering a sense of agency and resilience.

- **Healing and Growth:** Closure allows individuals to honor their past experiences and relationships, fostering healing and growth.
- **Inner Peace:** Finding closure gives individuals inner peace and resolution, allowing them to move forward with greater clarity and purpose.

EXAMPLE:

- **Michael's Letter:** Michael wrote a heartfelt letter to his estranged father, expressing his feelings and seeking closure. Although he never sent the letter, writing helped him process his emotions and find peace, allowing him to move forward. Through this process, Michael could honor his unresolved emotions and relationships, finding a sense of closure and inner peace.

Building a New Narrative: Reframing the Story of Estrangement

REFRAMING the narrative of estrangement is a transformative process that holds the potential to bring meaning and purpose to individuals navigating the aftermath of rupture. It involves a conscious shift from a narrative dominated by victimhood and loss to one characterized by resilience, growth, and personal agency. Through this reframing, individuals can reclaim their power and autonomy, transforming their experience of estrangement into an opportunity for profound growth and self-discovery.

At the core of reframing the narrative lies the emphasis on resilience. Despite the profound challenges and emotional turmoil associated with estrangement, individuals possess an inherent capacity for resilience. Acknowledging and highlighting their strength and resilience in adversity can cultivate a profound sense of empowerment and agency. Rather than succumbing to helplessness and despair, reframing the narrative empowers individuals to recognize their ability to adapt, persevere, and thrive despite even the most daunting obstacles.

Furthermore, reframing the narrative of estrangement involves seeking meaning and purpose amid adversity. Instead of viewing estrangement solely through the lens of pain and destruction, individuals can explore the more profound lessons and growth opportunities that emerge from their struggles. Every challenge presents an opportunity for growth and self-discovery, and estrangement is no exception. By embracing the inherent opportunities for personal development and self-awareness embedded within their journey, individuals can find purpose and fulfillment beyond the confines of estrangement.

ONE EFFECTIVE STRATEGY for reframing the narrative of estrangement is to focus on the growth and transformation that emerge from adversity. Despite the initial pain and upheaval, estrangement can catalyze profound personal growth and self-discovery. Individuals can explore how their experiences of estrangement have shaped their resilience, empathy, and capacity for self-reflection. By recognizing how they have evolved and grown as individuals, individuals can begin to view their experience of estrangement as an essential chapter in their journey toward self-actualization and fulfillment.

ADDITIONALLY, reframing the narrative of estrangement involves embracing the concept of post-traumatic growth. While estrangement undoubtedly presents significant challenges, it also allows individuals to cultivate resilience, gain clarity, and develop a more profound self-awareness. By reframing their experience of estrangement through the lens of post-traumatic growth, individuals can recognize how their struggles have catalyzed personal transformation and positive change. Rather than being defined by their pain and loss, individuals can emerge from the experience of estrangement stronger, wiser, and more resilient than ever before.

. . .

Moreover, reframing the narrative of estrangement entails shifting the focus from dwelling on the past to embracing the possibilities of the future. While it is natural to grieve the loss of relationships and the pain of estrangement, individuals can find solace and empowerment by directing their energy towards creating a fulfilling and meaningful life beyond estrangement. By focusing on their goals, aspirations, and dreams for the future, individuals can reclaim agency over their lives and cultivate a sense of purpose and direction that transcends the confines of estrangement.

Furthermore, reframing the narrative of estrangement involves challenging limiting beliefs and negative thought patterns that may perpetuate feelings of victimhood and helplessness. Individuals can explore how their beliefs about themselves and their relationships have shaped their experience of estrangement and work towards cultivating a more empowering and optimistic mindset. Individuals can develop a greater sense of self-worth, resilience, and agency by challenging negative beliefs and reframing their thoughts.

Benefits:

- **Personal Growth:** Reframing the narrative of estrangement encourages personal growth and self-discovery.

- **Empowerment:** Shifting from a victim mindset to one of resilience and strength fosters a sense of empowerment and control over one's life.
- **Meaning and Purpose:** Reframing the narrative helps individuals find meaning and purpose in their experiences, transforming adversity into an opportunity for growth.
- **Positive Outlook:** Reframing the narrative promotes a more optimistic outlook, fostering hope and resilience.

EXAMPLE:

- **Lisa's Transformation:** Lisa reframed her narrative of estrangement from her parents by focusing on her resilience and growth. Through therapy, she recognized her strength and ability to thrive despite the challenges, empowering her to pursue her goals with renewed determination. By embracing the opportunities for growth and self-discovery, Lisa transformed her experience of estrangement into a journey of personal transformation and empowerment.

Cultivating Inner Peace: Practices for Self-Compassion and Healing

FINDING inner peace amidst the turmoil of estrangement is a desirable outcome and a vital aspect of the healing process. It involves cultivating self-compassion and engaging in activities promoting emotional healing and well-being. Within the intricate landscape of estrangement, individuals often find solace and strength in mindfulness exercises, meditation techniques, and self-compassion practices, all of which serve as invaluable tools for nurturing inner peace and resilience.

MINDFULNESS STANDS as a cornerstone practice for those navigating the challenges of estrangement. At its essence, mindfulness involves paying deliberate attention to the present moment with openness and curiosity, free from judgment or attachment. By cultivating mindfulness, individuals can develop a heightened awareness of their thoughts and emotions, enabling them to respond to challenging situations with excellent stability and compassion. Through mindfulness practices such as deep breathing exercises, body scans, and mindful awareness of thoughts and sensations, individuals can anchor themselves in the present moment, fostering a sense of groundedness and inner peace amidst estrangement.

· · ·

Furthermore, meditation is a powerful practice for promoting inner peace and emotional healing in the wake of estrangement. By quieting the mind and turning inward, individuals can create a sacred space for self-reflection, relaxation, and rejuvenation. Meditation allows individuals to cultivate a deep sense of calm and tranquility, even amidst the storm of emotions that often accompany estrangement. Through regular meditation practices such as seated meditation, loving-kindness meditation, or guided visualization, individuals can nurture a profound sense of inner peace and resilience, enabling them to navigate the challenges of estrangement with grace and grit.

In addition to mindfulness and meditation, self-compassion practices are crucial in fostering inner peace and emotional well-being amidst estrangement. Self-compassion involves treating oneself with kindness, understanding, and acceptance, especially in struggle or suffering. It entails extending the same warmth and care to oneself that one would offer to a dear friend or loved one in need. Through self-compassion practices, individuals can cultivate a sense of inner resilience and strength, bolstering their capacity to weather the storms of estrangement with grace and compassion.

Self-compassion practices can take various forms, including gentle self-talk, acts of self-care, and moments of self-reflection and forgiveness. For instance, individuals can engage in positive affirmations, offering themselves encouragement and support in distress. They can also prioritize self-care activities that nourish their body, mind, and spirit, such as spending time in nature, engaging in creative expression, or connecting with supportive friends and loved ones. Additionally, individuals can cultivate moments of self-reflection and forgiveness, acknowledging their humanity and inherent worthiness and letting go of self-critical thoughts and judgments.

MOREOVER, self-compassion practices involve embracing the concept of self-acceptance, recognizing and honoring one's experiences and emotions without judgment or resistance. Rather than seeking to suppress or deny difficult emotions, individuals can practice radical acceptance, acknowledging and embracing the full spectrum of their feelings with kindness and compassion. Through self-acceptance practices such as journaling, expressive arts, or therapy, individuals can create a safe and nurturing space to explore their inner landscape, fostering healing and growth.

BENEFITS:

- **Emotional Stability:** Mindfulness and meditation practices promote emotional stability and reduce stress.

- **Self-Compassion:** Cultivating self-compassion fosters a nurturing and supportive relationship with oneself, promoting emotional healing.
- **Inner Peace:** Mindfulness, meditation, and self-compassion provide a deep sense of inner peace and resilience.
- **Healing and Growth:** Engaging in self-compassion fosters healing and personal growth, allowing individuals to navigate the challenges of estrangement with grace and resilience.

EXAMPLE:

- **Mark's Meditation:** Mark used mindfulness meditation to cope with the stress of his brother's estrangement. He developed excellent emotional stability and self-compassion through regular practice, helping him navigate his emotions more easily. By embracing self-compassion and mindfulness, Mark found inner peace and resilience, allowing him to move forward with clarity and purpose.

Moving Forward with Purpose: Setting Goals and Embracing New Beginnings

SETTING goals and envisioning a future beyond estrangement is crucial for healing and renewal. It involves identifying aspirations and taking concrete steps towards realizing them. By setting goals, individuals can create a sense of direction and purpose, helping them move forward with clarity and determination.

GUIDANCE ON BUILDING A SUPPORT NETWORK, pursuing interests and passions, and creating a fulfilling life can help individuals navigate the complexities of acceptance and closure. By surrounding themselves with supportive and understanding individuals, individuals can find comfort and validation in their experiences. Pursuing interests and passions can provide a sense of fulfillment and joy, offering a reprieve from the pain and sadness of estrangement. Creating a fulfilling life involves embracing new beginnings and opportunities, allowing individuals to cultivate a sense of purpose and meaning beyond the confines of estrangement.

ACCEPTANCE, closure, and moving forward are essential to the healing journey beyond estrangement. By embracing acceptance, individuals acknowledge the reality of their situation and let go of the hope for reconciliation. This process can be challenging, as it requires confronting the harsh truth that some relationships may never be repaired. However, by accepting this reality, individuals can free themselves from the burdens of the past and begin to move forward with their lives.

HONORING unresolved emotions is another vital aspect of the healing journey. By allowing themselves to grieve the loss of the relationship and express their feelings in healthy ways, individuals can begin to find closure and peace within themselves. This may involve writing letters to estranged loved ones, engaging in rituals to commemorate the end of the relationship, or seeking therapy to process their emotions.

REFRAMING the narrative of estrangement is also essential for finding meaning and purpose in the aftermath of rupture. Instead of viewing themselves as victims of their circumstances, individuals can emphasize their resilience, growth, and personal agency. By reframing their story, individuals can reclaim their power and autonomy, transforming their experience of estrangement into an opportunity for growth and self-discovery.

FINDING inner peace amidst the turmoil of estrangement is a vital aspect of the healing process. It involves practicing self-compassion and engaging in activities that promote emotional healing and well-being. Mindfulness exercises, meditation techniques, and self-compassion practices can all be valuable tools for nurturing inner peace and resilience.

. . .

ADDITIONALLY, setting goals and envisioning a future beyond estrangement can give individuals hope and purpose. By identifying their aspirations and taking steps towards realizing them, individuals can create a life filled with meaning, joy, and fulfillment, even in the aftermath of estrangement. This may involve pursuing education or career opportunities, building new relationships, or engaging in creative or philanthropic endeavors.

ACCEPTANCE, closure, and moving forward are essential to the healing journey beyond estrangement. By embracing these processes and taking proactive steps toward healing and renewal, individuals can create a life rich with meaning, purpose, and fulfillment. Through self-compassion, resilience, and determination, individuals can navigate the challenges of estrangement with grace and grit, ultimately finding peace and happiness amid adversity.

BENEFITS:

- **Renewed Purpose:** Setting goals and pursuing new interests gives individuals a renewed sense of purpose and direction.
- **Emotional Fulfillment:** Pursuing passions and

building a support network provides emotional fulfillment and joy.

- **Personal Growth:** Embracing new beginnings fosters individual growth and resilience.
- **Empowerment:** Setting goals and taking proactive steps toward healing empowers individuals to reclaim agency over their lives.

EXAMPLE:

- **Sarah's New Beginnings:** Sarah set new goals for her career and personal life after estranging herself from her family. She pursued her passion for art, joined a supportive community of artists, and found fulfillment in her creative endeavors. By setting goals and embracing new beginnings, Sarah created a life filled with purpose and joy, moving forward with renewed determination and resilience.

Using This Chapter to Move On

MOVING on from estrangement is a deeply personal journey that requires time, patience, and self-compassion. This chapter offers valuable insights and practical strategies for embracing acceptance, finding closure, building a new narrative, cultivating inner peace, and moving forward with purpose. By integrating these concepts and practices into their lives, individuals can navigate the complexities of estrangement with grace and resilience, ultimately finding healing and renewal.

EMBRACING ACCEPTANCE:

- **Acknowledge Reality:** Accept that some relationships may remain irreparably fractured despite your best efforts. Embrace the reality of the situation and let go of the hope for reconciliation.
- **Release Expectations:** Free yourself from unmet expectations and the emotional anguish of holding onto an elusive dream. Focus on your well-being and personal growth.

FINDING CLOSURE:

- **Honor Emotions:** Allow yourself to grieve the loss of the relationship and express your feelings in healthy ways. Write letters, perform rituals, or seek therapy to process your emotions.

- **Seek Resolution:** In the face of separation, find a sense of completion and finality. Embrace closure as a means of finding peace within yourself.

BUILDING A NEW NARRATIVE:

- **Reframe Your Story:** Shift from a narrative dominated by victimhood and loss to one characterized by resilience, growth, and personal agency. Recognize your strength and resilience in the face of adversity.
- **Find Meaning and Purpose:** Embrace the opportunities for personal development and self-awareness in your journey. Transform adversity into an opportunity for growth and self-discovery.

CULTIVATING INNER PEACE:

- **Practice Mindfulness:** You can develop a heightened awareness of your thoughts and emotions through mindfulness exercises and meditation. This will help you anchor yourself in the present moment and foster a sense of groundedness and inner peace.

- **Embrace Self-Compassion:** Treat yourself with kindness, understanding, and acceptance. Engage in self-care activities, positive affirmations, and moments of self-reflection and forgiveness.

Moving Forward with Purpose:

- **Set Goals:** Identify your aspirations and take concrete steps toward realizing them. Create a sense of direction and purpose in your life.
- **Pursue Interests and Passions:** Find fulfillment and joy in pursuing your passions and building a support network. Embrace new beginnings and opportunities.
- **Embrace Renewal:** Create a life of meaning, purpose, and fulfillment. Focus on your personal growth and resilience, and move forward with renewed determination and empowerment.

By following the guidance and strategies outlined in this chapter, individuals can navigate the challenges of estrangement with grace and resilience, ultimately finding healing and renewal. Embrace acceptance, honor unresolved emotions, reframe your narrative, cultivate inner peace, and move forward purposefully. You can create a life filled with meaning, joy, and fulfillment through self-compassion, resilience, and determination, even in the aftermath of estrangement.

BENEFITS:

- **Emotional Healing:** Integrating these concepts and practices into your life promotes emotional healing and well-being.
- **Personal Growth:** Embracing new beginnings and opportunities fosters individual growth and resilience.
- **Empowerment:** Reclaiming agency over your life empowers you to make decisions that prioritize your well-being and happiness.
- **Inner Peace:** Cultivating self-compassion and mindfulness fosters inner peace and emotional stability.

EXAMPLE:

- **David's Journey:** David used the strategies outlined in this chapter to navigate the aftermath of his parents' estrangement. By embracing acceptance, finding closure, reframing his narrative, cultivating inner peace, and moving forward with purpose, David created a life filled with meaning and fulfillment. He found healing and renewal through self-compassion and resilience, creating a life of purpose and joy.

Moving on from estrangement is a challenging but profoundly transformative journey. By embracing acceptance, finding closure, building a new narrative, cultivating inner peace, and moving forward with purpose, you can navigate the complexities of estrangement with grace and resilience, ultimately finding healing and renewal. Embrace the opportunities for growth and self-discovery, and create a life filled with meaning, purpose, and fulfillment. You can move forward with renewed purpose and empowerment through self-compassion, resilience, and determination, even in the aftermath of estrangement.

CHAPTER 7
BOOK REVIEW REQUEST

~

Make a Difference with Your Review

Unlock the Power of Generosity

==================================

"Sometimes the most ordinary things could be made extraordinary, simply by doing them with the right people." – Nicholas Sparks.

==================================

. . .

DEAR READER,

Thank you for taking the time to read "Estranged Relationships" by Michael Stevens. We hope you found the book insightful and thought-provoking. Your opinion matters greatly to us and future readers seeking understanding and comfort in their journeys with estrangement.

Why Your Review Matters

YOUR REVIEW CAN MAKE a significant difference. By sharing your thoughts and experiences with this book, you can help others decide if it's the proper read for them. Your insights might be the guiding light someone needs to navigate their complex relationships.

What to Include in Your Review

- **Your Overall Impression:** What did you think about the book? Did it meet your expectations?
- **Key Takeaways:** What are your main points or lessons from the book? How did it impact your understanding of estrangement?
- **Personal Connection:** Did any part of the book resonate with your experiences? How?
- **Recommendations:** Would you recommend this book to others? If so, why and to whom?

. . .

How to Leave a Review

LEAVING a review is simple and quick:

- **eBook Readers: Click on the Link -** https://www.
  amazon.com/review/create-review/edit?channel=
  glance-detail&ie=UTF8&asin=B0D34NQFS9

- **Paperback, Hardcover, or iPads:** Scan the QR
  Code -

- **Click on "Write a Review".**
- **Share your thoughts and give a rating.**

. . .

Spread the Word

FEEL free to share your review on social media or with friends and family who might benefit from reading "Estranged Relationships." Your recommendation can help others discover the book and gain the support they need.

THANK you again for your support and for being part of our community. Your review can make a meaningful impact.

WARM REGARDS,

MICHAEL Stevens

∼

CHAPTER 8

CONCLUSION: EMBRACING HEALING AND HOPE

~

Reflections on the Journey: Lessons Learned and Growth Opportunities

As we conclude our profound exploration into the intricate dynamics of estrangement, it becomes increasingly imperative to take a meaningful pause, allowing ourselves the space to reflect on the profound lessons unearthed throughout this transformative journey. Coping with estrangement is not merely a solitary ordeal but a profoundly personal odyssey, characterized by its tumultuous twists and turns, fraught with challenges that test the very fabric of our emotional resilience. However, amidst the stormy seas of estrangement, invaluable treasures of wisdom are waiting to be discovered, and opportunities for profound personal growth beckoning us to embrace them with open hearts and minds.

THIS JOURNEY HAS COMPELLED us to confront the complexities of estrangement with unwavering honesty and introspection, delving into the depths of our emotions and grappling with the complexities of fractured relationships. It has challenged us to confront our deepest fears and vulnerabilities, pushing us beyond our comfort zones and compelling us to confront the shadows of our past. Yet, amid this tumult, we have uncovered profound insights into human connection's intricacies and healing's transformative power.

MOREOVER, our exploration has illuminated the importance of empathy and compassion in navigating the tumultuous terrain of estrangement. In extending empathy to ourselves and others, we have fostered a deeper understanding of the complexities of human relationships and forged connections that transcend the barriers of estrangement. Through compassion and experience, we have bridged the chasm that divides estranged individuals, paving the way for reconciliation and healing.

OUR JOURNEY into the depths of estrangement has been a testament to the resilience of the human spirit and the transformative power of healing. It has challenged us to confront uncomfortable truths, navigate treacherous emotional waters, and confront the shadows of our past. Yet, it has also been a journey of profound growth, resilience, and self-discovery, offering us invaluable insights into the human experience and the transformative power of healing. As we bid farewell to this chapter of our lives, let us carry forward the lessons we've learned and the wisdom we've gained, embracing the journey ahead with hope, resilience, and an unwavering commitment to healing and reconciliation.

Personal Reflections and Insights

Each individual's journey through estrangement is as intricately unique as a fingerprint, intricately woven with the threads of their experiences, relationships, and emotions. As we take a moment to introspect upon the contours of our paths, we may uncover a rich tapestry of emotions—grief, anger, guilt, resilience, strength, and hope. Each emotion is an intricate weave in our lives, contributing to the richness and complexity of our narratives.

In the depths of estrangement, we have navigated the turbulent waters of grief, grappling with the profound sense of loss that accompanies the rupture of once-close relationships. We have tasted the bitterness of anger, fueled by perceived betrayals or unmet expectations, and wrestled with the weight of guilt, questioning our role in the breakdown of communication or connection. Yet, amidst the darkness, we have also discovered reservoirs of resilience within ourselves —resilience that has carried us through the darkest of nights and illuminated the path toward healing and reconciliation.

ALONG THE WAY, we have gleaned invaluable lessons that have reshaped the landscape of our lives. We have learned the importance of setting boundaries, recognizing our needs and limitations, and honoring them with unwavering commitment. We have prioritized self-care, nurturing our physical, emotional, and spiritual well-being with the tenderness and care it deserves. We have sought solace and support from trusted allies, finding strength in the embrace of those who support us on this journey.

IN THE CRUCIBLE OF ESTRANGEMENT, we have discovered the transformative power of forgiveness—the capacity to release the burdens of resentment and bitterness and embrace the liberating embrace of compassion and understanding. We have extended forgiveness to others, recognizing the inherent humanity and imperfection that defines us all, and forgiven ourselves for our own perceived shortcomings and mistakes. Doing so has unlocked the door to healing and reconciliation, paving the way for a future filled with hope and possibility.

. . .

As we reflect upon our reflections and insights, we recognize them as beacons of wisdom, guiding us forward on the path to healing and reconciliation. Each revelation is a stepping stone on our journey toward wholeness and restoration, reminding us of the resilience of the human spirit and the transformative power of love and forgiveness. As we continue to navigate the complexities of estrangement, may we carry these lessons as guiding lights, illuminating the path ahead with hope, resilience, and unwavering determination.

EMBRACING HOPE

In the aftermath of estrangement, hope often feels like a fragile flicker amidst the overwhelming darkness surrounding us. The pain of severed ties with loved ones can cast a long shadow, leaving us feeling lost, alone, and uncertain of what lies ahead. Yet, it is precisely in these moments of despair that hope reveals its true power—a beacon of light that pierces through the darkness, illuminating the path forward with its gentle glow.

In the face of estrangement's complexities, cultivating hope becomes imperative. Hope is the lifeline that keeps us afloat in the turbulent waters of grief and uncertainty, reminding us that even in our darkest moments, there is still the possibility of light. Hope beckons us to believe in the potential for healing, forgiveness, and renewal, envisioning a future where fractured relationships can be mended and broken hearts can find solace and peace.

BUT HOPE IS NOT MERELY a passive state of mind; it is an active choice that requires courage, resilience, and determination. It is the unwavering commitment to believing that better days lie ahead, even when the road ahead seems long and arduous. In the face of adversity, hope compels us to take action—to reach out to estranged loved ones, to extend the olive branch of reconciliation, and to do the hard work of healing and forgiveness.

HOPE IS the spark that ignites our resilience, giving us the strength to persevere in the face of seemingly insurmountable obstacles. It is the fuel that propels us forward, even when the journey is daunting and uncertain. Hope whispers words of encouragement in moments of doubt and despair, reminding us of our inherent worth and the boundless possibilities within our grasp.

MOREOVER, hope is not a solitary endeavor but a collective force that binds us together in solidarity and support. It is the shared belief that we are not alone in our struggle. Others understand our pain and are willing to walk alongside us on the journey towards healing and reconciliation. In embracing community and connection, hope finds fertile ground to take root and flourish, strengthening our resolve and renewing our spirit.

IN ESSENCE, hope is the thread that weaves through the fabric of our lives, connecting us to our past, grounding us in the present, and guiding us toward the future. The beacon of light leads us out of the darkness, reminding us that no matter how bleak the circumstances may seem, there is always reason to believe in the possibility of a brighter tomorrow. As we navigate the complexities of estrangement, may we hold fast to the transformative power of hope, allowing it to light our way and lead us toward healing, forgiveness, and renewal.

FINDING MEANING, PURPOSE, AND RENEWED STRENGTH

Estrangement, with its relentless upheaval and unsettling disruptions, has a profound way of stripping away the familiar anchors that once grounded us, leaving us untethered and adrift in an unfamiliar sea of uncertainty and loss. Yet, hidden opportunities for profound growth, transformation, and renewal lie amidst the void and disorientation. Within these challenging spaces, the seeds of resilience, hope, and inner strength are sown, waiting to be nurtured and cultivated.

. . .

EMBRACING hope amid estrangement's turmoil, we embark on a transformative journey of self-discovery and empowerment, reclaiming agency over our lives and forging a path toward a future filled with meaning, purpose, and fulfillment. Despite the overwhelming sense of disconnection and loss, we find within ourselves the capacity to cultivate hope, envision a brighter tomorrow, and take deliberate steps toward its realization.

IN THE WAKE OF ESTRANGEMENT, we may discover unexpected gifts and blessings amidst the pain and turmoil. Our journey through estrangement has sparked a newfound sense of purpose or reignited passions and interests long dormant within us. Navigating the complexities of estrangement reveals hidden strengths and resilience we never knew existed, tapping into inner reservoirs of courage and determination to overcome adversity.

MOREOVER, estrangement reshapes our relationships and deepens our connections with those who offer unwavering support and understanding. As we lean into the embrace of community support, we find solace in the companionship of loved ones who stand by our side, offering a lifeline of compassion and empathy amidst the storm.

. . .

Ultimately, embracing healing and hope allows us to transcend the pain and sadness of estrangement, emerging from the crucible of adversity stronger, wiser, and more compassionate than before. It is through embracing our experiences, finding meaning in our struggles, and nurturing the seeds of hope within us that we discover our capacity for resilience and renewal. In the face of estrangement's challenges, may we find the courage to embrace the transformative power of healing and hope, and may it guide us toward a future filled with possibility, growth, and abundant blessings.

Practical Steps Towards Healing and Reconciliation

While the emotional journey through estrangement is deeply personal, practical steps can be taken to facilitate healing and reconciliation. These steps are designed to provide a structured approach to navigating the complexities of estranged relationships and offer tangible strategies for moving forward.

1. Self-Reflection and Personal Growth: Reflect on your experiences, behaviors, and attitudes that may have contributed to the estrangement. This self-awareness is a crucial first step in understanding the dynamics at play and identifying areas for personal growth. Journaling, meditation, or seeking guidance from a therapist can be valuable tools.

THE ROLE OF JOURNALING: Journaling can be a powerful tool for self-reflection. Writing about your thoughts and feelings provides a safe space to explore your emotions, identify patterns in your behavior, and gain insights into the dynamics that contributed to the estrangement. This process can lead to greater self-awareness and clarity, helping you understand your needs and motivations.

MEDITATION AND MINDFULNESS: Meditation and mindfulness practices can help you stay present and grounded, reducing the emotional turmoil often accompanying estrangement. By focusing on the present moment, you can better understand your emotions and develop a greater sense of calm and resilience.

SEEKING THERAPY: Working with a therapist can provide valuable insights and support as you navigate the complexities of estranged relationships. A therapist can help you explore your feelings, identify areas for personal growth, and develop strategies for healing and reconciliation.

. . .

2. Setting Boundaries Establishing healthy boundaries is essential for protecting one's emotional well-being and maintaining self-respect. Clearly define acceptable behaviors and interactions and communicate these boundaries to others respectfully and assertively.

THE IMPORTANCE OF BOUNDARIES: Boundaries are crucial for maintaining healthy relationships and protecting emotional health. By setting clear boundaries, you can ensure your needs are met and treated with respect. This process involves identifying your limits, communicating them clearly, and enforcing them consistently.

COMMUNICATING BOUNDARIES: Effectively communicating boundaries requires clarity and assertiveness. Use "I" statements to express your needs and feelings, and be specific about what behaviors are acceptable and what are not. For example, you might say, "I feel hurt when you raise your voice during our conversations. I need us to speak calmly and respectfully to each other."

ENFORCING BOUNDARIES CAN BE CHALLENGING, especially if others resist or challenge them. Staying firm and consistent is essential, even in the face of pushback. Remember that setting and enforcing boundaries is an act of self-care and self-respect.

. . .

3. Prioritizing Self-Care: Engage in activities that nurture your physical, emotional, and mental health. These include regular exercise, healthy eating, sufficient sleep, mindfulness practices, and hobbies that bring you joy and fulfillment.

PHYSICAL SELF-CARE: Physical self-care involves taking care of your body through regular exercise, a balanced diet, and adequate sleep. These practices can improve your health and well-being, helping you feel more energized and resilient.

EMOTIONAL SELF-CARE: Emotional self-care involves nurturing your emotional health through activities that bring you joy and fulfillment. This can include spending time with loved ones, engaging in hobbies, or practicing mindfulness and relaxation techniques.

MENTAL SELF-CARE: Mental self-care involves caring for your mind through stimulating and challenging activities. This can include reading, learning new skills, or engaging in creative pursuits. Mental self-care can help you stay focused and motivated, enhancing your overall well-being.

. . .

4. Seeking Support: Contact trusted friends, family members, or a support group. Support offers empathy, validation, and practical assistance. Sharing your experiences with others who understand can provide comfort and reduce feelings of isolation.

FINDING A SUPPORT NETWORK: Finding a support network involves identifying people who can offer empathy and understanding. This can include friends, family members, or support groups. These individuals can provide a listening ear, a shoulder to lean on, and practical assistance as you navigate the challenges of estrangement.

BENEFITS OF SUPPORT GROUPS: Support groups can provide a sense of community and connection, offering a safe space to share your experiences and receive support from others who understand what you're going through. These supports also provide valuable resources and strategies for coping with estrangement.

PROFESSIONAL SUPPORT: Seeking professional support from a therapist or counselor can provide additional guidance and support. A therapist can help you explore your feelings, develop coping strategies, and navigate the complexities of estranged relationships.

· · ·

5. Professional Guidance: Consider seeking the help of a therapist or counselor specializing in family dynamics or estrangement. Professional guidance can provide valuable insights, coping strategies, and support as you navigate the complexities of your relationships.

FINDING THE RIGHT THERAPIST: Finding the right therapist involves identifying someone specializing in family dynamics or estrangement. Look for a therapist with experience working with individuals dealing with similar issues who can provide the support and guidance you need.

THE BENEFITS OF THERAPY: Therapy can provide space to explore your feelings, gain insights into the dynamics of your relationships, and develop strategies for healing and reconciliation. A therapist can also help you build resilience and coping skills, enhancing your overall well-being.

TYPES OF THERAPY: Various types of therapy, including individual therapy, family therapy, and group therapy, can be beneficial for dealing with estrangement. Each offers unique benefits and can provide valuable support as you navigate the complexities of estranged relationships.

. . .

6. Support Communication: When you feel ready, initiate open and honest communication with the estranged individual. Approach the conversation with empathy, active listening, and a willingness to understand their perspective. Avoid blame and focus on expressing your feelings and needs constructively.

PREPARING FOR THE CONVERSATION: Preparing for the conversation involves identifying your goals, setting boundaries, and planning what you want to say. Consider writing down your thoughts and feelings to help you organize them and stay focused during the conversation.

ACTIVE LISTENING: Active listening involves entirely focusing on the other person, showing empathy, and responding thoughtfully. This can help create a safe space for open and honest communication, fostering understanding and connection.

EXPRESSING FEELINGS AND NEEDS: Expressing your feelings and needs involves using "I" statements to communicate your emotions and what you need from the other person. This approach can help avoid blame and create a more constructive and collaborative conversation.

. . .

7. Forgiveness and Compassion: Work towards forgiving yourself and others involved in the estrangement. This process may take time and include acknowledging the pain and anger you feel. Practicing compassion towards yourself and others can pave the way for healing and reconciliation.

THE POWER OF FORGIVENESS: Forgiveness is a powerful tool for healing and reconciliation. It involves letting go of resentment and anger and embracing compassion and understanding. Forgiveness does not mean condoning harmful behavior but instead releasing the emotional burden it carries.

PRACTICING **Self-Compassion** involves treating yourself with kindness and understanding, especially during difficult times. This can help you navigate the emotional challenges of estrangement and build resilience.

EXTENDING COMPASSION TO OTHERS: Extending compassion to others involves recognizing their humanity and imperfections and approaching them with empathy and understanding. This can create a more positive and supportive environment for healing and reconciliation.

8. Rebuilding Trust: Trust is often damaged in estranged relationships, which requires consistent effort and patience.

To rebuild trust, restore confidence, demonstrate trustworthiness, maintain open communication, and acknowledge and amend past mistakes. Trust can be rebuilt gradually through small, consistent actions over time.

BUILDING TRUST **through Consistency** Building trust involves demonstrating reliability and consistency in your actions and behaviors. This can help create confidence in safety and predictability, fostering trust and connection.

OPEN COMMUNICATION: Maintaining open and honest communication is crucial for building trust. This involves being transparent about your feelings and needs and actively listening to the other person's perspective.

ACKNOWLEDGING MISTAKES: Acknowledging and amending past mistakes is essential in building trust. It involves taking responsibility for your actions, making amends, and committing to positive change.

9. Creating New Narratives: Reframe your experience of estrangement to promote healing and growth. Identify the lessons learned, the strengths developed, and the new perspectives gained. Use this new narrative to guide your future actions and relationships.

. . .

THE POWER OF REFRAMING: Reframing involves changing how you perceive and interpret your experiences. This can help you find meaning, change your struggles, and create a more positive and empowering narrative.

IDENTIFYING LESSONS LEARNED: The lessons learned from your experience of estrangement can help you gain valuable insights and wisdom. This can guide your future actions and relationships and promote personal growth and resilience.

EMBRACING NEW PERSPECTIVES: Embracing new perspectives involves being open to change and growth and recognizing the potential for positive transformation. This can help you navigate the complexities of estrangement with greater clarity and confidence.

10. Embracing Change: Accept that relationships may not return to their previous state and that change is a natural part of growth. Embrace the opportunity to create new, healthier dynamics reflecting personal growth and insights gained through the estrangement journey.

. . .

THE NATURE OF CHANGE: Change is inherent in life and relationships. Embracing change involves recognizing its potential for growth and transformation and being open to new possibilities.

CREATING NEW DYNAMICS: Creating new dynamics involves establishing healthier patterns of interaction and communication that reflect your personal growth and insights. This can help create more positive and fulfilling relationships.

EMBRACING the journey involves recognizing that healing and reconciliation are ongoing processes. Be patient with yourself and others, and celebrate the progress you make along the way.

～

Encouragement for the Journey Ahead

AS WE PREPARE to close the chapter on estrangement, I want to extend a heartfelt word of encouragement to all of you who have embarked on this challenging yet profoundly transformative journey. It's essential to recognize that healing is not a straightforward path; it's more like a winding road filled with unexpected twists and turns, moments of clarity and confusion, triumphs and setbacks.

· · ·

As you navigate this journey towards healing and reconciliation, I want to remind you to be gentle with yourself. Feeling a whirlwind of emotions—sadness, anger, confusion, and even moments of hope and joy is okay. Embrace these feelings with open arms, knowing they are all valid and a natural part of the healing process.

Remember that you don't have to walk this path alone. Reach out to trusted friends, family members, or a supportive community who can offer a listening ear, a shoulder to lean on, or a comforting presence during difficult times. Seeking support is not a sign of weakness; it's a courageous step towards healing and growth.

And in those moments when the darkness feels overwhelming and hope seems out of reach, hold onto that flicker of hope with all your might. Even when it feels like shadows surround you, remember there is always a glimmer of light somewhere, waiting to guide you through the darkness.

Together, we can navigate the complexities of estrangement with courage, resilience, and compassion. By honoring our emotions, seeking support when needed, and holding onto hope, we can emerge from this journey with renewed strength and a deeper appreciation for the intricate tapestry of human connection. So, as we bid farewell to this chapter, let us embrace the journey ahead with open hearts and unwavering determination, knowing that healing and reconciliation are possible and within our reach.

Final Thoughts: A Future of Healing and Connection

As we conclude this exploration of estrangement, let us carry forward the lessons, insights, and hope we have cultivated along the way. While profoundly challenging, estrangement offers us the opportunity for profound personal growth, transformation, and the renewal of our most cherished relationships.

May we approach the future with compassion, forgiveness, and unwavering hope. Let us embrace the possibility of healing for ourselves and those with whom we have been estranged. By fostering empathy, practicing open communication, and nurturing our well-being, we can pave the way for a future filled with meaningful connections, mutual understanding, and lasting reconciliation.

Together, we can transform the pain of estrangement into a catalyst for growth, resilience, and profound healing. As we move forward, let us hold onto the belief that no relationship is beyond the possibility of renewal and that the journey towards healing, though arduous, is one of the most rewarding paths we can undertake.

May the journey ahead be one of hope, strength, and boundless possibility as we embrace the transformative power of healing and the enduring promise of reconciliation.

CHAPTER 9

FURTHER READING AND RESOURCES

~

I n this chapter, I would like to provide a curated list of additional books and resources that delve deeper into estrangement, healing, and personal growth. Whether you're seeking more in-depth insights, practical advice, or stories of resilience, these books offer valuable perspectives and guidance to support your journey. The authors featured in this chapter, including Dr. S.M. Stinnette, Dr. Jennifer Michaels, and Michael Stevens, have all dedicated their work to helping individuals navigate complex emotional landscapes and find pathways to healing.

Books by S.M. Stinnette

"THE MINDSET RESET- REPROGRAMMING YOUR BRAIN FOR A BETTER LIFE: LASTING CHANGE AND PERSONAL GROWTH THROUGH SELF-TRANSFORMATION"

"THE MINDSET RESET" is ideal for anyone seeking significant and lasting changes. Whether you want to improve your career, relationships, health, or overall well-being, this book offers valuable insights and practical tools to help you achieve your goals and unlock your full potential.

"EMOTIONAL INTELLIGENCE: THE PATH TO SELF-AWARENESS AND PERSONAL GROWTH"

"Emotional Intelligence: The Path to Self-awareness and Personal Growth" is a comprehensive guide that delves into the transformative power of emotional intelligence in shaping our lives. From understanding the intricate dynamics of self-awareness to fostering personal growth, this book offers invaluable insights into harnessing the profound impact of emotions on our thoughts, behaviors, and relationships.

"RESILIENCE UNLEASHED: THRIVING THROUGH LIFE'S CHALLENGES"

In this transformative book, you'll discover practical strategies for navigating setbacks, overcoming adversity, and thriving amid life's uncertainties. Through inspiring stories of triumph over adversity, you'll gain insights into the psychology of resilience and learn how to cultivate a resilient mindset.

Books by Dr. Jennifer Michaels

"ANXIETY RELIEF: STRATEGIES FOR MANAGING STRESS, IMPROVING EMOTIONAL HEALTH, AND INCREASING SELF-CONFIDENCE"

DR. JENNIFER MICHAELS offers a practical guide to overcoming anxiety. The book includes strategies for managing stress, improving emotional health, and boosting self-confidence.

Books by Michael Stevens

"HOW TO BE CHRISTLIKE: A JOURNEY OF FAITH, TRANSFORMATION, AND LEGACY"

IN A WORLD YEARNING for genuine love, compassion, and integrity, "How to Be Christlike" offers a transformative guide to living a life that reflects the character and teachings of Jesus Christ. This profound and practical book invites readers to embark on a lifelong journey toward Christlikeness, fostering spiritual growth, personal development, and impactful living.

"EXPLORING CHRISTIANITY: A JOURNEY OF UNDERSTANDING"

"Exploring Christianity: A Journey of Understanding" is more than a mere intellectual exercise; it is a pilgrimage of the soul, an odyssey of faith, and a testament to the enduring power of belief. As we embark on this voyage together, may we find illumination in the shadows, wisdom in the mysteries, and unity in the diversity of the Christian experience?

THESE BOOKS SERVE as valuable companions on your healing and personal growth journey. They offer diverse perspectives and practical strategies to help you navigate the complexities of estrangement, cultivate inner peace, and build healthier relationships.

BIBLIOGRAPHY

Coleman, J. (2016). When Parents Hurt: Compassionate Strategies When You and Your Grown Child Don't Get Along. William Morrow Paperbacks.

McBride, K. (2012). Will I Ever Be Good Enough?: Healing the Daughters of Narcissistic Mothers. Atria Books.

Forward, S. (2003). Toxic Parents: Overcoming Their Hurtful Legacy and Reclaiming Your Life. Bantam.

Scharp, K. M., & Thomas, L. J. (2018). "Interpersonal forgiveness, relationship quality, and communication in the parent-adult child relationship." Journal of Family Communication, 18(2), 107-121.

LaRocco, D. J. (2019). "Understanding the dynamics of parent-adult child estrangement." Journal of Divorce & Remarriage, 60(2), 117-133.

Robinson, L., & Segal, J. (2021). "Estranged Adult Children and Their Parents: A Psycho-Social Perspective." Journal of Family Issues, 42(10), 2398-2419.

Merriam-Webster. (n.d.). "Estranged." Retrieved from https://www.merriam-webster.com/dictionary/estranged

Stand Alone. (n.d.). "Support for Estranged Adults and Those Who Love Them." Retrieved from https://www.standalone.org.uk/

Dr. Jennifer Michaels, Clinical Psychologist, Personal Interview, 02/2020, 04/2024.

Dr. S.M. Stinnette, Clinical Psychologist, Ph.D. in Neuroscience, Personal Interview, 02/2020, 04/2024.

U.S. Department of Health and Human Services. (2017). "Family Estrangement: Recommendations for Practitioners." Retrieved from https://www.hhs.gov/programs/social-services/family-support/strategies-for-improving-family-relationships/family-estrangement/index.html

ABOUT THE AUTHOR

∼

Michael Stevens, the esteemed author of "Estranged Relationships: What Can Be Done—Is There Anything to Be Done?" is a respected theologian and spiritual guide known for his insightful exploration of Christian faith and dedication to fostering healing and reconciliation in personal relationships.

While Michael is renowned for his contributions to Christian theology, "Estranged Relationships" represents a deeply personal departure from his typical literary endeavors. Drawing from his experiences of navigating the complexities of estrangement, Michael brings a unique blend of personal insight and spiritual wisdom to his exploration of fractured relationships and the journey toward reconciliation.

Throughout his career, Michael has demonstrated a profound commitment to promoting empathy, understanding, and forgiveness in his personal and professional life. His work is characterized by a deep reverence for the transformative power of faith and the importance of compassion in fostering healing and renewal. This commitment is sure to inspire readers on their own journey toward healing and renewal.

As a prolific writer and speaker, Michael has touched the lives of countless individuals with his heartfelt messages of hope and reconciliation. His unique ability to blend personal narrative with spiritual insight makes his work not only relatable but also a guiding light for readers seeking direction on their journey toward healing and renewal.

Through "Estranged Relationships: What Can Be Done - Is There Anything to Be Done?" Michael Stevens shares his deeply personal story of estrangement and redemption, offering readers hope and a roadmap for navigating the complexities of fractured relationships with faith, compassion, and resilience. Michael invites readers to heal and reconcile with courage, honesty, and grace, reminding us of the transformative power of love and forgiveness in restoring broken bonds.

Chapter One Publishing Company, LLC.
    https://chapter1-publishing.com
    Facebook:
    https://www.facebook.com/profile.php?id=
61561990586022

~

ALSO BY MICHAEL STEVENS

∾

"How to Be Christlike: A Journey of Faith, Transformation, and Legacy"

"Estranged Relationships: What Can Be Done - Is There Anything to Be Done?"

"Understanding Christianity: Exploring the Depths of Faith"

"Exploring Christianity: A Journey of Understanding"

Also Michael Stevens

Michael Stevens, the esteemed author of "Estranged Relationships: What Can Be Done—Is There Anything to Be Done?" is a respected theologian and spiritual guide known for his insightful exploration of Christian faith and dedication to fostering healing and reconciliation in personal relationships.

While Michael is renowned for his contributions to Christian theology, "Estranged Relationships" represents a deeply personal departure from his typical literary endeavors. Drawing from his experiences of navigating the complexities of estrangement, Michael brings a unique blend of personal insight and spiritual wisdom to his exploration of fractured relationships and the journey toward reconciliation.

Throughout his career, Michael has demonstrated a profound commitment to promoting empathy, understanding, and forgiveness in his personal and professional life. His work is characterized by a deep reverence for the transformative power of faith and the importance of compassion in fostering healing and renewal.

As a prolific writer and speaker, Michael has touched the lives of countless individuals with his heartfelt messages of hope and reconciliation. His ability to blend personal narrative with spiritual insight makes his work relatable and inspiring for readers seeking guidance on their journey toward healing and renewal.

Through "Estranged Relationships: What Can Be Done - Is There Anything to Be Done?" Michael Stevens shares his deeply personal story of estrangement and redemption, offering readers hope and a roadmap for navigating the complexities of fractured relationships with faith, compassion, and resilience. Michael invites readers to heal and reconcile with courage, honesty, and grace, reminding us of the transformative power of love and forgiveness in restoring broken bonds.

"Understanding Christianity: Exploring the Depths of Faith"

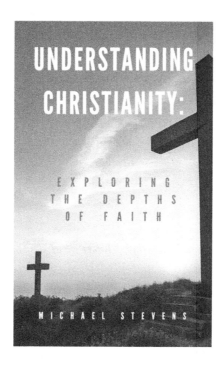

Dive into the depths of faith with "Understanding Christianity: Exploring the Depths of Faith." This captivating journey invites you to unravel the mysteries, embrace the wisdom, and discover the transformative power of Christianity.

In this illuminating exploration, you'll journey through the history, theology, and spirituality of one of the world's most influential religions. From the ancient teachings of saints and scholars to the vibrant expressions of faith today, this book offers a comprehensive guide to understanding Christianity in all its complexity and beauty.

Whether you're a seasoned believer, a curious skeptic, or a spiritual seeker, "Understanding Christianity" promises to inspire, challenge, and enlighten. With engaging storytelling, profound insights, and practical wisdom, this book will surely deepen your understanding of the Christian faith and enrich your spiritual journey.

Join us on this extraordinary adventure as we delve into the heart of Christianity and uncover its timeless truths. Pick up your copy of "Understanding Christianity: Exploring the Depths of Faith" today and embark on a voyage of discovery that will transform your life forever.

∽

"Exploring Christianity: A Journey of Understanding"

"Exploring Christianity: A Journey of Understanding" sets sail on a voyage of discovery, navigating the currents of history, theology, and spirituality to uncover the hidden depths of this ancient faith. Like intrepid explorers charting uncharted territories, we embark on a quest to unravel the layers of Christianity, peeling back the veils of time to reveal its origins, evolution, and enduring significance. Along the way, we encounter saints and sinners, martyrs and mystics, theologians and reformers whose lives witness the transformative power of faith.

From Jesus' humble birth in a Bethlehem manger to the global spread of his message of love and redemption, the story of Christianity is one of resilience, transformation, and transcendence. Alongside its triumphs, however, are shadows of complexity— doctrinal debates, historical controversies, and ethical dilemmas— that challenge believers and scholars alike. In this journey, we grapple with the enigma of the Trinity, ponder the mysteries of salvation and atonement, and wrestle with the ethical imperatives that underpin Christian morality.

At the heart of Christianity lies the profound mystery of the Triune God—Father, Son, and Holy Spirit—whose nature transcends human comprehension yet invites us into a relationship of love and communion. We have explored the theological implications of this mystery, grappling with concepts such as divine omnipotence, omniscience, and omnipresence and pondering the significance of the Trinity in the life of believers.

"Exploring Christianity: A Journey of Understanding" is more than a mere intellectual exercise; it is a pilgrimage of the soul, an odyssey of faith, and a testament to the enduring power of belief. As we embark on this voyage together, may we find illumination in the shadows, wisdom in the mysteries, and unity in the diversity of the Christian experience? As we contemplate the mystery of the Trinity, we are reminded of the boundless depths of God's love and the call to live in unity and harmony with one another.

∽

"How to Be Christlike: A Journey of Faith, Transformation, and Legacy"

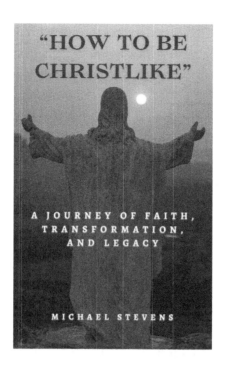

"HOW TO BE
CHRISTLIKE"

A JOURNEY OF FAITH,
TRANSFORMATION,
AND LEGACY

MICHAEL STEVENS

"How to Be Christlike: A Journey of Faith, Transformation, and Legacy" embarks on a transformative odyssey, guiding us through the rich tapestry of Christian life. This book charts a course through the essential elements of faith, examining the teachings, virtues, and practices that define what it means to follow in the footsteps of Jesus Christ. Like devoted disciples traversing the landscape of discipleship, we delve into the essence of Christlikeness, uncovering the timeless wisdom and transformative power embedded in His life and message.

From the humble beginnings of Jesus' ministry in Galilee to the far-reaching impact of His teachings across the globe, the narrative of becoming Christlike is one of profound personal and communal transformation. Alongside the joys and victories of faith, we also confront the trials and tribulations that test our commitment and integrity. In this journey, we explore the profound concepts of grace, mercy, and forgiveness, and we wrestle with the call to love unconditionally, serve selflessly, and live justly in a complex and often challenging world.

At the heart of Christlikeness lies the call to embody the virtues of humility, compassion, and love. We examine how these virtues are not merely ideals to aspire to but practical experiences that shape our daily interactions and decisions. By embracing these Christlike attributes, we are invited into a deeper relationship with God and one another, fostering a community rooted in the love and teachings of Jesus.

"How to Be Christlike: A Journey of Faith, Transformation, and Legacy" is not just an intellectual pursuit; it is a journey of the heart and soul, a path of transformation that impacts every facet of our lives. As we travel this path together, may we find inspiration in Jesus' example, strength in our shared faith, and hope in the legacy we are called to create? This journey challenges us to reflect on our actions, attitudes, and aspirations, continually seeking to align our lives more closely with the example set by Christ. Through this process, we are reminded of the enduring power of faith to transform individuals and communities, leaving a legacy that echoes through generations.

Made in the USA
Las Vegas, NV
09 October 2024

96590047R00148